HOW TO FALL APART

From Breaking Up to Book Clubs to Being Enough – Things I've Learned About Losing and Finding Love

Liadán Hynes

HACHETTE
BOOKS
IRELAND

First published in Ireland in 2020 by
HACHETTE BOOKS IRELAND

2

Cataloguing in Publication Data is available from the British Library

ISBN 9781529381214

Typeset in Sabon by redrattledesign.com

Printed and bound in Great Britain by
Clays Elcograf S.p.A

Hachette Books Ireland policy is to use papers that are natural, renewable and recyclable products and made from wood grown in sustainable forests. The logging and manufacturing processes are expected to conform to the environmental regulations of the country of origin.

Hachette Books Ireland
8 Castlecourt Centre
Castleknock
Dublin 15, Ireland

A division of Hachette UK Ltd
Carmelite House, 50 Victoria Embankment, EC4Y 0DZ

www.hachettebooksireland.ie

HOW TO FALL APART

Liadán Hynes is a journalist who lives in Dublin with her five-year-old daughter. She writes for a number of publications including the *Sunday Independent*, the *Irish Independent*, *Irish Tatler* and *Image*, and had a weekly column for Image.ie titled *Things Fall Apart* about being a single parent and putting life back together after separation.

Liadán is also the host of *How to Fall Apart: a podcast about picking up pieces*, examining how people coped, or didn't cope, during the difficult times in life. She is a founding member of online publication *rogue*, which features writing, video and podcasts by Irish creators.

For Sarah, the biggest joy bringer of them all.
I love you to the sun, moon, stars and back
– times infinity.

Prologue

'Nobody goes into a marriage thinking it will fall apart.'

I say this to my friend Sophie.

'Really?' she says. 'I needed to know that I could have an out before I could do it.'

We both laugh – because, of course, she's joking.

Mostly.

But also because it's the kind of thing you say when you have a lovely, solid marriage, so you can comfortably take the odd pot-shot at it.

All four of my best friends – Sophie, Shereen, Rachel, Nikki – have lovely marriages. It's the kind of thing I sometimes feel should be upsetting. Because I did have a lovely marriage. And now I don't. It's the sort of thing that should press up against the bruise of the fact that I am getting a divorce.

Nobody goes into a marriage thinking it will fall apart.

I think part of the reason I don't find it upsetting is that I did, once, have a lovely marriage. But I have accepted it is over, and I don't long for something I no longer have.

But that acceptance is not the only reason.

It's also because when you get up close to other people, you realise that, while they may not have a broken relationship or marriage, there will always be something that they have had to carry, or had to fix.

And it is because of what these women have done for me over the past few years as my marriage fell apart. Listened, advised, persisted when I didn't reply, always answered when I called out of the blue.

Carried me.

So I could never feel envious of them. 'Sister-wife', Sophie and I joke about one another sometimes. And I, who have no real sisters and am no longer a wife, claim them as such.

When you break yourself open, in the way that a marriage falling apart will make you do, you realise that you are made up of all kinds of things – you are not just that one relationship that seemed to be the foundation of everything else.

Nobody goes into a marriage thinking it will fall apart.

I was never one of those people who dreamed about her big day. I think this is probably because whatever my own parents said about their 'big day' (a phrase they would never have used) was casual of tone at best. A floral maxi dress for my mother; a cord blazer for my father. A ring bought the day before in a market which she has lost – and replaced – regularly over the years. A casual wedding. But a lovely marriage.

Nobody goes into a marriage thinking it will fall apart.

When my husband and I first met, in our early twenties, he was late and I was cross.

Despite this unpromising beginning, we both seemed to know almost instantly that there would be an us; that this was in some way a foregone conclusion.

A given thing.

I watched him as he walked to the car and told myself 'I can't possibly go out with a man in brown cord flares'. My next thought: 'the flares would have to go'. That I was going to go out with him was an assumption I had not even noticed myself making.

He later told me that at the end of our second meeting he thought, 'I'm going to marry her.'

Several weeks into us knowing each other, my friend and flatmate Rachel and I threw a house party specifically to get him to the house. Eager to confirm his attendance, I rang him ten times while his phone was off to invite him.

Little did I realise that even off, his phone would show up the missed calls. Coming out of a meeting I picked up a voice message. 'Hi. I'm not sure if everything is OK. I seem to have missed a number of calls from you. Ten, I think.'

Ten.

Even through the haze of mortification that almost led me to drop the phone I could hear the gentle amusement in his voice.

We had the party. And he came. And he managed, as I got to know him, to be that rare thing to a single woman in her twenties. A man not off-puttingly interested (needy), not toyingly cold (game playing), just straightforward.

He was funny, and sweet, and kind. He regularly got up at four in the morning to drive his mother to the airport.

And it was easy, in the way that it is when you meet the right person. In that way that makes you realise how ill-fitting all those other stop-and-start relationships really were. How they could never have worked, because this is how it should feel. We were both on the same page, wanted the same things. Wanted each other the same amount.

We went on holidays. We moved in together. Adopted a cat.

'You're so much nicer now', my mother teased me. I was so much happier.

When his mother fell terminally ill, I watched as he minded her in hospital with such care and tenderness it almost broke my heart.

'I'm so glad this is the person I will grow old with,' I thought.

Almost two years later, we got married in a church made of corrugated tin beside a lake, where our guests stayed in yurts, and we fed them barbecued burgers and cake, and we danced under bunting made by aunts and cousins.

And while I did lose myself just momentarily in fussing over seating arrangements and table decorations, I knew the real point in getting married. We were already committed to each other; getting married was a step that meant that we would have a child. Our wedding led to our daughter. So, even though the marriage wasn't lovely in the end, even though things fell apart, in one way, they are exactly as they should be, what we agreed to be on that day. We are parents to our daughter.

Nobody goes into a marriage thinking it will fall apart.

Nobody does all the things that knit you together so tightly – the minutiae that make up a life; the Sunday-night takeaways, the minding each other through hangovers, the trips to IKEA. Nobody finds a man who when you look at him you realise *oh yes, I do want to have babies after all. His babies*, and thinks it will fall apart.

Nobody finds a person who seems to be the best friend to trump all others, the person you turn to in the middle of the night because you cannot sleep with the worry, with whom conversation never runs dry, and thinks that, in years to come, you will sit in separate rooms in the evening, with nothing to say to each other.

Nobody has a baby with someone and thinks that within four years you will live under different roofs.

Nobody goes into a marriage thinking it will fall apart.

We used to tell each other how lucky we were to have found each other, because it fit so easily. And I thought that we would grow old together; gardening and grandchildren.

But one day you look around and realise you don't recognise your life anymore. Where has all the stuff that made your marriage so wonderful gone, you think? And you see that your life is closing down. And that there is a previously unimaginable wedge between you.

And that you cannot find your way back to each other.

When a marriage ends, people often say, 'Thank God there were no children involved'. But when my marriage ended, I thanked a God I don't believe in for our child. A child made it harder to end things, but easier to bear when they did end.

When the midwife announced at the five-month scan that we were having a girl, I thought, *We've won the lottery*. I hadn't even admitted to myself how much I wanted our baby to be a girl. A girl, who is, in herself, a happy ending.

It is not the ending I imagined, but it is more than enough in its own way. As happy an ending as any. For this child is pure love. A person with the ability to make it all OK, even at the times when it really wasn't.

*

Of course, the real saying is that nobody goes into a marriage thinking it will *fail*. But I do not think of the end of my marriage as a failure. When you have tried so hard to make something work and then, finally, faced that fact that it won't. That sometimes people change and all the counselling, all the talking, nothing will fix this. When you have faced into the scariness of that, that doesn't feel like failure.

*

Nobody goes into a marriage thinking it will fall apart.

But sometimes things do just fall apart.

And then you put them back together.

And if you are lucky, like I was, you don't have to do it on your own.

Your people will pick up your pieces.

Part One

Things Fall Apart

Chapter 1

Facing the Music

The knowledge that your marriage is over isn't something that settles on you in one moment. It isn't like a light bulb – nothing one minute, full illumination the next. Unless, of course, one of you has gone off and made the decision on your own. That is different.

Sometimes, it comes as a slow, creeping dread that steals gradually upon you. You might know it in some hidden part of your being. It is there at some level, but you have not yet been able to admit it to yourself.

Because realising your marriage is over is terrifying. It's like a death. Not just the death of the future you had planned – the realisation of that will come – at the start, it is the death of life as you know it right in this moment. It feels unnatural. To break with your existing life, tear it all down, even if a part of you knows it is the right thing to do. Unnatural, and oh so terrifying.

It's sort of a mundane loss, a break up, given most of us will experience it at some point in our lives. But I can't think of another which so comprehensively flattens your whole life as you know it; the loss of the person you share it with. When my college boyfriend and I broke up, it was shocking how easily our lives untangled, even though we had been together for some time. But losing the person you have lived with for years?

It changes everything from the moment you open your eyes each day. How your house sounds, what food you eat, how you will raise your child. What part of your bed you sleep in.

'You'd be surprised how deep denial can go,' a health-care professional told me months after we separated. *No I wouldn't,* I think.

When you are deep in this denial, sometimes you need someone who can, ever so gently, point it out to you.

There aren't many people who could say to you, 'I think your marriage might be in trouble', and you wouldn't immediately rear up in defensiveness, unable to hear what they were saying, because you were too lost in your angry reaction, ignoring the words and just feeling furious and attacked.

It takes a very particular type of relationship to be able to broach that one. You need people who can speak the absolute truth to you, and you will listen.

Not curl up in a ball and shut your ears, all prickly like a hedgehog. People who are so fundamental to you, so much a part of you, that they can get beyond your defensiveness.

Because you do not need to be defensive with them. You can show them the worst side of you, and there's no pride to be protected here. The flipside is that you get to believe them when they tell you that you will be OK. Because everyone here is being honest, brutally so or otherwise.

I was lucky, I had two such people: my mother and my oldest friend, Shereen.

I first spotted Shereen the day we started secondary school, both of us were twelve.

She was sitting behind and slightly above me, in the stepped tables of a small science classroom. I noticed her because she was laughing loudly with her then best friend, and I felt a flash of irritation that was actually jealousy; I wanted to be in on her laughter.

We were in the same class, so it didn't take long for us to get to know each other and, pretty soon, we were best friends.

As teenagers, we fought with an at times epic sense of drama. 'It's like watching bloody Heathcliff and Cathy,' Claire, a more even-tempered member of our gang of five, muttered one night, after watching Shereen run out of a sleepover and take off down the road, me dashing after her, half to coax her back, half to continue the row.

Claire was right though. These were the impassioned rows of a big love. I look back now and realise we were fighting with the security of two people who knew, even at the age of twelve, that they were givens in each other's lives. Who could really let loose with one another. If you do not like confrontation (and I don't), it can mean you need to feel very safe in a relationship before you will test it out by rowing with a person. I have only ever rowed with my mother with an impunity, scale and sheer abandon similar to that with which Shereen and I faced each other during those teenage years.

We always rowed over differences of opinion. 'No, *you* are wrong and *I* am right.' You row with someone like that because they matter to you, and what they think about things matters to you.

Some people have bitchy resting face. Shereen has stern resting face. She is no-nonsense. If I need total honesty, I know she will give it to me. And I will seek it from her as I might not with others; there is no pride getting in the way. I can trust her entirely.

When things are coming to an end, she happens to be home from London. It is the summer, our twenty-year school anniversary. We go, but sit in the dark corner ignoring everyone, while I fill her in. 'Of all my friends, you are the one I know can get through this,' she tells me. And even though part of me thought it was just a nice, comforting thing to say, another part of me, because I know Shereen does not say things for the sake of it, holds it close, and uses it to get me through, like a buoy grabbed on to at sea.

Shereen thinks I can do this. I can do this.

Chapter 2

Let It Go

When she was two and a half, my daughter and I went with my friend Sophie and her eldest son Roo to a singalong screening of *Frozen* in the cinema. We took the DART to Dún Laoghaire, our first time travelling by train, which was exciting in itself, and had pizza and ice-cream in Milano's afterwards. It was Christmas.

In the cinema, Elsa's big number comes on the screen and my daughter stands up, arms thrown wide, a tiny opera singer, singing fiercely, *con brio*. She has all the moves down: her hands flutter as she creates Olaf, the finish a dismissive flick of her imaginary plait. Sophie, Roo and I watch on in admiration. 'She knows all the words,' Sophie mouths across behind her, impressed. And she did, even if she didn't understand all of them. I am ridiculously proud.

Looking back now, I think Elsa was singing to me. It just took me a while to hear her properly.

Let. It. Go.

How do you know when it is time to let go of the life you had planned? To end a marriage?

Particularly when there is a small child involved and the decision doesn't really feel like it is fully yours to make. Because whatever you decide will affect the outcome of someone else's life so entirely as well. How do you carry the weight of such a decision?

With all this in mind, how do you know when to let it all go?

Is it when you find yourself having a stilted conversation about the weather with someone you considered to be your best friend? Someone with whom it was previously inconceivable that conversation would ever run out?

When something happens, and you realise that the first person you want to talk to about it isn't your husband, it's your best friend.

When you say you miss each other, but then you realise that what you both really mean is that you did miss each other, but now, almost without realising it, you have begun moving on.

When you have done the months of counselling, the date nights, the holidays – all of it – and yet things are still not right, not the way they were or the way they should be.

When you realise that you feel lonely in the company of the person you promised to love and cherish forever more.

When you find yourself thinking, *We could stay together until she is eighteen,* and realise what you would say to a friend if she said that to you.

Is it when your mother tells you that it will all be OK, everyone will get through this – that your daughter will be fine, more than fine, and you believe her. Because you know she holds your daughter's welfare as closely as you do, and that she is a terrible liar and you would know if she was faking it. It frees up something deep within you, gives you a sort of permission, to begin edging towards the decision.

'Why don't you just stop trying?' Shereen said.

'She will be alright,' my mother said.

In their different ways, both are saying *let go*. Stop trying to force this situation to your will. Give in. It will be OK.

'Everything will work out,' my mother said ever so gently. And even the fact that she can imagine it ending gives me hope. Someone else to whom this matters almost as much as it does to you thinking the worst before you can face it yourself lifts the burden a little. Makes you think, *Well, if they can face it and believe that things might be OK, then maybe I can too.*

After so long of trying, and ignoring, and fearing, and pretending, this is happening, let's deal with it, was her attitude. *Your daughter will be OK*. Which, we both knew, meant that I would, too.

When you are faced with having to pull the cloth

out from under the set table of your life, and two of the people who know you best and know you longest look you calmly in the eye and say, 'It's time. It's the right thing to do. You can do this. She will be OK. You will be OK ...' You believe them.

And it means you *can* do it.

If you're at that point in your own life, and you're full of fear – the kind of fear that makes you sick to your stomach, that hits you first thing in the morning before you even leave your bed – know that you can do it.

Know that sometimes, the ripping off of the plaster is the worst part.

Few things are worse than stasis. Than knowing deep down in your bones, that the most intimate fabric of your life is rotten, and not facing it. Knowing that the foundations upon which you have built your life are giving way, but that you are too scared to do anything about it, because it feels too awful to face.

Throughout the collapse of my marriage, few things were worse than the fear that I felt at this point.

At least in facing what is happening, you are taking action. Creating momentum. There is power in that. It may not feel like it at the time, but you are taking back control of your life. Saying, 'This is not good enough, this state of affairs. For me, for her, for him, for all of us.'

And with this comes the relief in letting go. In

admitting that things are just not working. All the anger and frustration that was going into trying to keep things together dissipates. Some of it turns into energy that you can use to move forward.

And while it might not feel like it right at that moment, there is power in no longer trying to control the outcome. You are saying to yourself, '*Whatever* happens, I can handle it. I will be OK.'

In the first months after we separated, I used to imagine the three of us in the air, thrown up by a huge trampoline. My daughter clung to my chest like a baby koala; her father and I with our arms outstretched towards each other, sometimes only our fingertips touching. No longer a couple, would always be parents. Helpless, unable to bring ourselves back down to earth, forced simply to wait it out.

Control was non-existent. But at least we were moving, rather than stuck in the silent scream. At least we were facing it.

'In a way, you're taking a risk when you're letting go,' Lou, my yoga teacher, and one of the wisest women I know, tells me much later. 'There's crippling fear; letting go is terrifying. But in letting something go, you create more space for life. For growth.'

And, in that moment, when you admit to each other that the relationship is over, that it is time to let go, you are kind to each other. You are heartbroken, you are dazed. But at least you are not angry.

Chapter 3

How to (Re)build a Home

A short time after we have decided our marriage is over but before my husband has moved out, we are sitting together on the couch one night, watching *Game of Thrones*. This doesn't happen often by this stage – us sitting together. The show makes a strangely appropriate backdrop with which to see out the closing chapters of a marriage. It's almost reassuring. Well at least we're not *that* bad. All those other families, tearing themselves to pieces. And at least it can be relied upon not to offer up some happy ending that will throw our own situation into sharp relief.

Apart from raising our daughter, it is the last thing we see through together. We committed to the marriage, but that didn't work out. We have committed to *Game*

of Thrones, and we will see that out – or until the end of the seventh series at least.

He has moved out long before the eighth began, and I haven't been able to face watching it with someone else. I read the spoilers.

Having decided that you will watch a certain show with someone, watching it with someone else – or, even worse, alone – simply will not do. When my college boyfriend and I broke up we were deep in the second series of *24*, hardly able to get through the day quick enough before returning home to see what obstacle Jack Bauer would have to overcome next. And then we broke up, and I never watched the end of Kiefer Sutherland's tortuous day. All of a sudden, I didn't care.

As we're sitting there, together, but really not together at all, I am hit by a wave of panic and claustrophobia that seems to come out of nowhere. It suddenly feels as if the walls of my cosy, redbrick terraced house are closing in on me, while the ceiling is telescoping rapidly upwards. All of this is happening at terrifying speed.

I am in a tunnel. A cell.

The words 'this is your cell' actually flash across my mind.

A vision of the countless nights to come, sitting on my couch alone, my daughter upstairs asleep, follows quickly to further scare me. Thoughts of being trapped here, while life goes on around me outside. It feels more terrifying than anything I have ever known. As if my life, or any control over it, has been taken from me. Contact with anyone will cease at my child's bedtime. Silence will reign thereafter. I will sit alone while, outside, everyone else gets on with their lives. Life will pass me by. I am Miss Havisham, only I am decaying away in a small redbrick terraced house by the sea.

I consider what age I will be before she is a teenager, and I no longer need to sit here, on guard, keeping silent watch, night after night. See my life slipping quietly away in front of me, counted out in evenings spent alone and silent on my L-shaped IKEA couch. Think of the person and the age I am now, and the person and age I will be when this sentence of solitude ends.

Chapter 4

A Day Out

You can know that your marriage is in terminal trouble but also know that there is a lot about your life that you love.

My brother's girlfriend Song Yue came home from China where she has been on holiday – actually, she is Chinese, China is her home, but so comprehensively have we taken to her in our family that I now think of our home as hers. My girl has adored her from the first; Song Yue is a daughter whisperer.

Song is calm and quiet and, like our childminder Po, just the sight of her makes me feel reassured.

I can do this, if we are surrounded by people who love my daughter like she is their own, I think, beginning a bargaining process with myself. People who create a safety net around us.

When you are in the process of breaking up their world in some way, knowing your child is surrounded by people who love them like family is very comforting.

'Your non-negotiables,' a friend says much later, when life has come back around to being something I feel I can shape and exercise some control over, rather than something I have to suffer through white-knuckled, and the thought of having non-negotiables, of being able to decide that certain things are essential to my life, is beginning to seem possible.

'I *suppose* Mommy is the love of my life,' my daughter tells my brother one night as he puts her to bed. She says it in a considering voice; she will allow me the distinction. 'And Song of course,' she adds quickly.

We decided to go to Malahide on the DART to celebrate Song's return. My daughter sits opposite Grandad (my father, but so entirely has he inhabited the role of grandfather that this is how we now all refer to him). They play with L.O.L. dolls on the ledge of the window.

'So handy for a day out,' my mother says approvingly of their diminutive stature. Like me, she is not a fan of fantasy play. 'I've done my time playing on the floor,' she says, adding that my father 'loves it' in a tone that will brook no suggestions to the contrary. Her title, bestowed by my daughter, is 'Mo'. It started when she began calling her 'Mum', copying me. *This could get weird,* I thought, but, after a few days, she turned it into 'Mo'. Again, this is what the whole family now calls my mother.

I sit back on my seat and allow things to wash over and around me, my family to occupy my daughter. She kneels up on her chair, looks over at me, beaming delightedly.

When we arrive at the park, my daughter can't quite believe it, a real live castle. 'I should have worn my Elsa dress,' she says, throwing me a reproachful look at having allowed this missed opportunity.

It's a surprisingly warm, sunny day. We sit on the grass eating cakes, taking turns to go for more coffees and chasing my daughter, her mop of curls springing up and down as she runs away from us screaming with laughter. I'm let off going for coffee runs; my marriage is falling apart, I couldn't possibly be expected to have to deal with a queue.

My marriage may be over but there is so much of my life I love, I think as I watch them. It feels entirely baffling that these two things could even be possible, never mind entirely true.

Doublethink; the act of simultaneously accepting two contradictory beliefs.

Cognitive dissonance more like; the mental discomfort of holding two contradictory beliefs – because holding these two thoughts at once is certainly not comfortable.

Chapter 5

The Woman from the Future

A few weeks before he moved out, I attended a work dinner with a lot of other journalists. We were seated at a long, candlelit table and the PR, who is one of the best in Dublin, much admired and so in receipt of a huge turnout for her event, had been very clever about her seating arrangements.

Everyone down one side of the table was in their early twenties, probably no one over twenty-five. They spend the evening switching between ignoring their fellow guests, hunched over their phones, furiously tapping away, and posing with each other, rictus smiles in place.

They seem to take no offence in the huddled silence of their neighbour in between the picture-taking during which they hold each other close, heads tilted together. They interact only when posing for their respective selfies. It's an odd communication gap I see all around me in the media world; women who can communicate intimately, gregariously with their thousands of followers in videos on their Instagram stories, but for whom small talk, IRL, leaves them stumped. You ask them question after question but things never get off the ground into an actual conversation. The lost art.

On the other side are women mostly in their thirties and upwards, who have known each other for years by dint of working in the same industry. As the evening goes on, chairs get dragged over into little groups. For this side of the table, this is a chance to catch up. Face to face.

Beside me is a woman I know and like from a distance. She is someone who invites instant intimacy and straight talking. As the conversation buzzes around us, I lean in and ask her quietly: 'How is it – living on your own?'

She looks a bit shocked, and as if she might be on the edge of taking offence at such nosiness.

I quickly explain that this is not idle nosiness. 'I'm about to start doing it myself. In the next few weeks.'

There isn't much in adult life I can think of that compares to how I feel when I am on the brink of my marriage ending. It's as if my life is about to drop off a cliff – and I have no idea into what. I'm sailing out to sea towards the unknown, all alone.

Maybe the woman beside me spots this, my need for reassurance, the feeling of being utterly at sea in my own life, because her whole body relaxes, and she smiles. 'Mostly, it's grand, but it takes a bit of getting used to,' she says reassuringly, and asks me to go for brunch the following weekend.

Chapter 6
The Fear

When your marriage or long-term relationship falls apart, it can take away your sense of safety and leave you with an ever-present sense of fear.

Partly, I think it is the simple fact of being so all-systems-over-burdened that you fall prey to the fear, because you don't have the strength you normally would have with which to fight it off. It's like a cloud that hovers above, and you are all hairline fractures, so fear easily slips in and takes up residence.

But it's more than that.

'Do you mean insecurity?' a friend asks me this when I try to describe this fear. I had used the word 'safe' – how your sense of safety goes. I know she thinks I mean insecurity about being alone, being single. But that's not what I mean.

Divorce is a trauma that isn't considered (typically) to endanger your physical health (at least not in any one fell swoop; long-time stress sufferers might disagree) – but it is a trauma and, as such, undermines your sense of safety in the world.

'You're traumatised,' my friend Lewine says to me one day. We first met at a mother and baby group where we bonded in the face of our children's refusal to sleep. Now, we're at a play café, fending off our children with endless rounds of snacks so we can catch up. I would never have said it about myself because it would have felt self-dramatising but now, it feels like every molecule in me bristles in recognition of the truth of her words.

Loss takes away a sense of safety you didn't realise you had until it becomes obvious by its absence. You realise your assumption of life as a safe place was founded on nothing.

The fear also comes from the fact that, no matter how amicable a separation is, there will be times when things become heightened between you. Being at odds with the person who was once your ultimate safe space, however mildly, undermines your peace of mind and ability to feel secure in your own life.

And there is the fear caused by the future you imagined disappearing before your eyes. *What do I do now?*

Chapter 7

Ships in the Night

When a marriage gets to the point of breaking down, chances are things have not been good for some time. In our case, it was a mutually agreed détente, but even for those for whom the decision is announced as a fait accompli out of the blue, you look back and see that there were little signs that something was wrong.

Little ways in which your homelife had become less than what you wanted for you both – what you once actually had. Compromises you have made, gradual acceptances of things being a certain way. You may not have been screaming at each other, but the atmosphere was, at the very least, not right.

Perhaps there were strained conversations where once there was only ease.

Discussions that batted back and forth only between the essentials of getting through a day – food to be bought and prepared, children to be tended to, who had last emptied the dishwasher and would you take out the bins. All that, without the other ways of communicating to leaven the brass tacks. The chatting in bed, the watching a movie together.

Two people shuffling awkwardly around each other, each in their own bubble of isolation.

In our case, a heavy storm grounds the entire country for several days just before he moves out. If you want to know if your marriage is really over, spend four days trapped with the other person in a small two-up two-down house. You might be surprised by how quickly the place becomes a pressure cooker.

You know how even when you're happily married to someone, you occasionally want to rip their head off? How you can go from nought to a hundred in minutes because of some small household chore left undone? Imagine that ability to get under each other's skin, the ignorer of boundaries that is the intimacy born of marriage or a long-term relationship, in the atmosphere of two people who have decided to leave each other. Bone-dry tinder, just waiting for a spark.

In the end, we negotiate a sort of truce, moving our daughter back and forth between our two zones as we take turns working, avoiding each other as best we can. And yet, as always, our daughter manages to make things better. In a break in the weather, she suggests playing outside, and a no-man's land is established in the back garden. She and her father dress in layers, while I watch from the door taking photographs. Are we pretending things are OK for our child – or are things, on some level, OK *because* of our child? She is a buffer between us and the worst.

Chapter 8

Moving Day

He moved out on a Tuesday, a day that seemed insufficiently momentous.

I doubt, though, that any day of the week would rise sufficiently to the occasion. It seems unlikely that there is a time at which it would seem fitting to watch your husband pack up his things and move out of the home you have both shared for a decade.

Watching his belongings go into boxes feels surreal. A backward step that is against the nature of things. These items are not made for moving; this house is where they live. Except now, they don't. It turns out that even the most tightly meshed of lives can be pulled apart. When he moved in, before we got married, we bickered amicably over paintings and cushions. Now we are gentle with each other over what will go or stay.

Who really cares about a bloody lamp anyway?

While he packs up, I whisper down the phone to my friend Sophie from the farthest corner of the house. Which, given this is a two-up two-down, means the next room. She suggests coming over, but I save her offer of company for nights in the future, when I know I will need her.

I'm not really sure how to do this. Even though I cry down the phone, there is a flipside. Relief, to be moving to the next stage. It feels deeply wrong to admit to it, but there is a rush of relief that comes out as a sort of effervescent celebratory amicability between us. We are relieved to be moving to the next stage.

Ideally, you would break up with a person and that would be it. Say goodbye and never see them again, and then face going about the task that at times seems almost unimaginable. To set about making a stranger of the person you have known better than anyone else. All that time spent building an intimacy, come to nothing.

Having a child together means this is not possible. You must find a way.

But when it actually comes to the 'living apart' part, you may both be ready for it to a certain extent.

Ready to be separate. Even though this is not how you thought things would turn out, and you are more sad about how things have turned out than you are yet ready or strong enough to admit, there is a certain relief in your home not being a battleground. Instead, it becomes a place of refuge.

It is both a shock and a relief, to be alone.

Separated, the house becomes both a sanctuary and then, very gradually, a statement of intent about my new life.

*

I take to sleeping in my daughter's bed. Just for this first week, I tell myself, while things feel particularly odd and bereft. I never leave. It seems ridiculous for the two of us to be in separate rooms throughout the night when she, not yet four, is so little, so hot-water-bottle like.

The two of us curl up in her bed as in a nest, the impenetrable darkness of a child's blackout blinds providing the ultimate sense of escape from the world. 'What is your place of total peace of mind?' I'm asked months later at a meditation course. 'My daughter's bedroom, on a Friday night. She's asleep, I'm reading, the following morning holds no commitments.'

Chapter 9

A Tell All

I didn't expect that telling people would take as much out of me as it did. Surely the separation was the big deal. I presumed telling people would be relatively straightforward. I was wrong.

We waited. Waited for it to settle within us. Until it was possible to say the words and not feel the shock of it course through us all over again, to accept that this had happened to us. I remember hearing of friends who had been separated for six months before they told anyone and wondering why they kept it a secret for so long.

Now, I got it.

Partly, putting off 'the telling' is a form of self-protection. You need to get yourself to a place of being

OK before you're ready to trot it out for the world to see. You need to be a bit gathered, a bit robust.

This is, in part, because, at its worst, the telling can lead to you counselling others through *their* shock at the turn of events. Having to sit through their performance of grief. 'It's so saaaaaad,' they will wail.

Believe me, I know, you will think. *But I'm having a good day, so let's not invite in the sadness, shall we?*

Back then, I guarded my good days with a zealousness bordering on the obsessive, knowing how fragile they were. 'How practised have I become at living in the now?' I would tell myself smugly, on a good day. '*Look at me, Mum*,' I think, '*practically Eckhart Tolle*.'

'We're past the worst of it.' A phrase I trotted out on a regular basis. A trite little truism that I used to block any further queries. One day, much later, I said it yet again, and realised that that time it was true.

When you tell people about a difficult thing that has happened, their reaction will go one of two ways. They may be sympathetic, but pitying. They will see you and your sad stuff as something other – maybe a little scary, definitely to be pitied. They will tilt their heads, pucker up their mouths, make a pitying moue.

I call them the 'head-tilters' – all the women I interview for my podcast *How to Fall Apart* recognise this description instantly with a slightly irritated roll of their eyes. No one wants to be pitied.

Then there are the empathisers, those who just get it.

They're not afraid of the bad stuff, probably because they have had a taste of it themselves, either of loss or of a life that has gone off the rails of the expected. Their attitude it that this is bad but that this is also life, and we will deal with it.

Attach yourself to these people. They will lift you up.

The main difference between the two, I think, is fear. Chances are the head-tilters have yet to experience the inevitable – that, at some point, life will pull the rug out from under you. The latter know this and have coped with their own experiences. 'If it hasn't got you yet, it's coming for you,' Sophie and I say to each other of the head-tilters, laughing conspiratorially. Maybe it's not though.

When I interview her months later, Elizabeth Gilbert tells me that if life hasn't made you suffer, good for you, keep on going – but if it has, come sit with me.

Seeing the reaction of the head-tilters sort of forces you to relive a little bit of the horror and sadness of the news all over again. 'No, no,' I want to tell them impatiently. 'We've done this. We're already five miles down the road. You're at *entirely* the wrong stage of grief. It's all fine. We're at acceptance; get on the right page, please.'

As if you can decide when, and how quickly, you are done with grief and its stages. I know better now.

Some are better at learning bad news than others.

Some, by their reaction, will lift you up. Reassure you that what has happened is bearable and not an un-come-backable-from fissure in the fabric of life. Other reactions are just to be got through, tolerated. With these people, I try to be brisk with their shock – it is not mine to carry, it is theirs – I have my own.

The reactions of some people are truly awful. Two friends wait months, then text to say: 'I was so sorry to hear, and I'm so sorry I'm only getting on, I simply didn't know what to say.' Never do this. Telling someone you could not find the words with which to address their life will only make them feel like their life is simply too dreadful to even contemplate.

Some people in my life are harder to tell than others. I can't face telling the aunts and cousins, so my parents do it for me. I don't want to see their sadness for me, which is kind, not pitying. They handle it perfectly, sending texts that are supportive, not maudlin. Offering food shops, weekly to-be-taken-up-at-the-last-minute dinner invitations. My aunt sends a care package; a book of essays by Irish women, a Terry's Chocolate Orange, a bottle of prosecco, and an instruction to take a night off for myself and sit and consume all three. Genius.

Again, I feel like a ball shot into the air but this time my family act as the ledges of a pinball machine, catching me, slowing down my descent so that I do not crash.

I handle some of my attempts to tell people badly, out of sheer awkwardness. At a breakfast with schoolfriends ostensibly to admire a new extension, I start to say it when half of them are across the other side of the now large kitchen. They do not hear me, and then I am crying, and have to half shout the news across the room, while the others at the table signal frantically for their attention. 'WE HAVE SEP-AR-AT-ED.'

Dreadful. But also very funny, as dark things often are with people you have known all your life.

I tell two friends in the middle of a playdate at my house, as five children of various ages run screaming at various volumes around us. I am feeling OK about things, a bit nonchalant even, a fact that naturally throws them, given the juggernaut of news I have just unloaded out of the blue. News that we must then discuss in coded language and part whispers, amidst the noise of the children dashing around us.

I become an expert at spelling the word 'separated', and then almost too familiar, I constantly forget. Three *e*s or two *a*s?

I tell one group of friends by text. We had planned a day out at a hotel for facials and afternoon tea, but suddenly I could not face the idea of the whole day of planned pampering becoming about my life, this breakdown of things. So, I cancelled by text, and spent the day in bed, hiding under the duvet. The right move. If nothing else, a life crisis gives you the ability to bow out where before you might have made yourself push through.

And then there are the people you do not get to tell. The ones you love, but who are on your ex's side, his family. And you wonder what they think, whether they are shocked or secretly suspected because amongst them are the people who knew you best as a couple. The people you thought you would go on holiday together with for years, watch your children play and grow together.

Some of them send texts out of the blue: 'We love you. We will always be family.' It's almost too painful to reply.

Having read every account out there on these things, I can say with some authority that telling your parents that your marriage is over is often almost as hard as the break-up itself. Almost a second break-up, with all sorts of horrible things involved – shame, feelings of failure, the shouldering of their grief.

I am lucky that there wasn't really a telling when it came to my own parents. They saw it all as it unfolded, from right inside the bubble that was breaking.

I suspect, in fact, that my mother knew before I did.

Either way, their only reaction was to say that everything would be OK. That my daughter would be OK. When your life as you knew and had planned it is collapsing around you, having those two people look back at you with absolute calm and say that everything will be OK, and keeping all their fears and upset to themselves is the most generous gift they can give you.

Chapter 10

The Trauma Map

There is a thing called the 'Trauma Map', a sort of tool used by mental-health professionals to illustrate what we can go through when something bad happens. Laid out on paper, it is a number of boxes, connected by lines. The biggest box represents you, your day-to-day, normal self. Beside it is another big box. This is your animal, reactive self.

The self that is triggered when something bad happens to you, and you suffer trauma.

Below these two big boxes are a number of smaller ones, all sorts of reactions to trauma which can kick in. Fear, fight (anger), flight (avoidance), freezing, please and appease, and detachment. At worst, these reactions can take over, become like a mini personality.

In fact, the real you is still in there, you just need to find your way back.

What helps you back can be a mixture of things. You own pre-existing levels of resilience. Your support network, how connected you are to other people. The work you do on yourself to stay in as good shape as possible mentally, the rituals and habits – meditation, yoga, sport, reading, spending time with friends, counselling – whatever is your practice to maintain wellbeing (a sense of peace of mind, of things being well and manageable in your life).

Trauma will probably happen to all of us at some point or other. You need to find the things, or the people, who will help you find your way back.

'Back' might be the wrong word, as you will be changed by the trauma you have experienced. 'Through' may be a better word, through to a new you.

I had had nothing close to trauma in my life until my marriage ended. Now, I needed people to help me find my way through. People who would catch, hold and then propel me. Help me to feel safe again. People who would help me figure out how the hell to find my way through this and get to the other side. Navigators who, at times, became the actual ship.

Chapter 11

A Haven to Hide In

I don't think anybody *wants* to start counselling. Going for the first time is terrifying. Because, chances are you have been keeping a lid on quite a lot before you go for your first session. You may be trying to pretend it doesn't exist – this stuff under the lid – but, of course, you know it does, even if you have yet to examine it closely and are in no rush to do so.

Much better to continue on, if not in blissful ignorance, then in uncomfortable denial.

Opening it all up to examination is not tempting. In fact, it might seem almost impossible because you are barely managing to keep things going as it is. You have nothing left over to give to examinations – where will you find the energy to wade in and start trying to fix things?

We had started going to Helen the counsellor when we were trying to save our marriage. Now that it is over, I go back to her on my own. Driving out the first time, alone, feels like one of the saddest things I've ever done.

But, similar to acknowledging the marriage was over, very quickly going to counselling felt like taking things in hand in a way that seemed closer to empowerment than to fear. 'You are stronger than you think,' Helen told me on my first solo visit, which may be a cliché all counsellors tell new patients, but it worked.

My mother had found Helen through a friend who is on a board. She comes highly recommended, specifically, the friend tells my mum, 'If it were me, if it was my marriage, this is who I would go to.' She is a talker, rather than a mute listener, an approach I couldn't have coped with. She will give me her opinion, or some modicum of it, when I ask. And by opinion, I really mean advice.

Something about her room comforts me instantly. I think it is the fact that it shares many of the trappings of my grandparents' living room, where I would lie on the couch on sick days if my mother had to work, and be fed Corn Flakes with sugar, ice-cream with melted raspberries from their garden, and watch *Blockbusters* and *Neighbours* with my gran. Like that room, Helen's office has heavily daubed oil paintings of forest scenes framed in dark oak and a soft pink lamp with a tasselled shade. More homey than clinical.

If I let myself think too much about it, it could feel sad – me and Helen still sticking it out; my husband gone. This was the place we had come to piece things back together, only that hadn't worked. And here I still was.

But really, this is a place of comfort. First and foremost, Helen is kind and her room is a haven. She never ends a session abruptly on the hour, always allows things to come to a natural close, so that we leave on an upward note. 'I see what you're doing,' I say one evening, months in. She has asked me to name a few of the things I think I am doing well, just before it is time to leave. 'You're making sure I leave here on a high note.'

She smiles to herself in acknowledgment.

Going to Helen doesn't feel at all like emptying the contents of myself in a way that is painful. In fact, it feels like having someone guide and help me through this, someone who can be relied upon to give fair, expert advice. A strategist. A navigator.

In one corner of the office, a low coffee table is covered in crystals that remind me of the glass paperweights scattered about my gran's house. They are never mentioned except when called upon to perform as actual people; Helen, momentarily a sort of military general, lays them out on the floor – a brown-and-orange patterned carpet, also grandparental – working out a plan, a strategy for life, each crystal representing a person.

I have to cross the city to get here; it's a round trip that can take over three hours.

My friend Nikki, who I worked with straight out of college, and who is now married to my cousin, lives around the corner from Helen, and the route to this office is the same as to Nikki's house. Another cousin and an aunt also live nearby. Places I visited long before coming to Helen, so being here often feels like I am on a social visit.

The office above a doctor's surgery, this area, becomes the centre of what I later come to think of as my Bermuda Triangle of recovery. Helen, Judith the theologian, and the yogi Lou – the three women who will help put me and my life back together again, all situated within several streets of each other. Each the powerful pinpoint of a space within which I bounce back and forth, looking for a way out. A way to mend, to be now, afterwards.

They create a map.

Chapter 12

How to be an Angry Woman

I sit in Helen's room and she smiles politely, listening to me.

'Anger does not serve me', I am saying. Perhaps a shade piously. Definitely delusionally.

But I genuinely believe what I am saying. 'What is the point in anger?' I ask Helen rhetorically. It seems like such a waste of time. And I really believe that I am not angry, anyway. No one has had an affair, our marriage has just reached a mutual ending. And there is so much of my life that I love. My daughter, being a mother. My family, my friends, my work. Why waste my time on anger when I can be getting back to enjoying those things? I just want to try as best I can to get on with life.

So, anger is pointless. A one-way street. Not even, a cul de sac. A waste of time going in, an emotional dead-end. I'll skip it, thanks all the same. I'll be over here, moving on.

Anger feels like the opposite of going forward. The stuff of futility. Of whining and railing at the unfairness of life. Dwelling. Resentful. Ruminating. All circular, dead-end emotions – and I, for one, wasn't going to be indulging in it.

Of course, what Helen knows, but I don't yet, is that it's not anywhere near as simple as that.

Because, of course, I don't get to decide these matters. To pick and choose which emotions I will and won't dabble in (be almost drowned by, more like). It seemed pointless to me, to allow anger to exist within me. As if the allowing was within my power. As if I could decide what, and when, I would feel.

When your life implodes, you do not get to choose your reactions. Or when you are going to have those reactions. This is probably the most exhausting thing about it all. About grief. The absolute lack of control over how you will feel in the space between getting up and going back to bed. The up-and-down nature of your days.

The best you can do is to go with it, and tell yourself that the more you allow the reactions to pass through you, the quicker, and more permanently, you will get back to your own self.

The stages of grief do not play out in real life like tidy stepping stones, one after the other, in a manageable, predictable sequence. Dealt with once, then gone forever. But they must all be dealt with, usually more than once. Usually, relentlessly, again and again until you give in and stop saying you're done with them, and just wait it out until they're done with you. This is necessary, if acceptance – that holy grail of grief – is ever to be reached.

'That's a hard one,' my doctor tells me one day when I go to him having self-diagnosed vitamin B deficiency. 'What else is going on?' he asks casually, never a man to rush to a prescription. I tell him, and he gently suggests that the fact that I keep feeling like I'm going to pass out might be, is in fact, stress, not a vitamin deficiency. 'Many people get really stuck before getting to acceptance,' he says. 'They never quite make it. Or it takes them years. Decades.'

Helen knows all this, so she smiles politely, kindly, as I assure her that anger is not for me.

Because of course I am angry. Of *course* I am. Angry that my life has not gone the way I had planned. That this has happened to me. To my family. My daughter.

I'm so angry I have to unfollow several perfectly harmless people on Instagram because I can't stand the sight of their allegedly perfect lives. Not even heavily filtered lives, just modest, 2.4, nuclear-family lives.

So angry that, for months, I cannot fully turn my

head to the right, cannot look over my shoulder, because my neck has seized up with a rage I'm not letting myself admit to.

So angry that, sometimes, when I sit down to meditate, boiling waves rise up from my deepest depths, and I feel like I might be consumed by them. I'm amazed by how much I can deny of what is within me.

I am angry for rational reasons, and angry for irrational ones.

'The things is,' Helen says gently, in a pause between my monologuing, 'the thing about anger is that it's quite like music. It comes to a crescendo. So loud it can feel unbearable. Scary even. As if it might capsize you. As if you can't quite cope with it. As if it might be too much for you to bear. And then it passes.'

It always passes.

It passes through you. But it only does that when you allow yourself to feel it. If you don't feel it, you will never let it out. And it will sit within you, twisting up the muscles of your back and neck. Vice-gripping your temples into crippling headaches. Turning your stomach so you wake up feeling sick and run for the bathroom, but nothing comes. Putting you on a fuse so short that any little thing can make you snap. Even though, of course, you are not angry. What would be the point of that?

I am so angry that, at one point, I punch a window.

It is a calculated act of anger, done to shock. An

attempt to use my anger for my own benefit. Three seconds before my hand hits the window, I am assessing what speed my fist needs to hit the glass with to ensure the real impact I'm trying to make here – shock value, but not enough to actually hurt myself.

I am full of rage. I am also exact; neither hand nor window are in any great danger.

I write about it later in my column, 'Things Fall Apart'. But, in that, I say I punched a wall. I discuss it beforehand with Sophie and my mother. We decide that the image of punching a window is somehow too shocking and will make people think of broken glass, torn skin and blood.

We all know that we need to tread gingerly around that so unpalatable a thing – an angry woman. Because an angry woman is an out-of-control woman, a hysterical woman, a mess.

Which makes anger so bloody difficult for women to process. An angry woman is 'hysterical', 'raving', 'neurotic', 'out of control'; an angry man is 'impassioned', 'strong', 'threatening', 'powerful'. 'Sad' seems like an acceptable emotion for a woman. For a mother. Soft, sorrowful, but in some way cleansing too. And purposeful. Washing things out of my system. Anger is violent. Punchy – literally, in my case – a bit scary. Capable of warping me.

And physically very uncomfortable, a sort of burning in the throat, tightening of the back, clenching of the jaw and swirling in the stomach.

Who wants to be an angry woman? I certainly didn't.

Chapter 13

The Cloud

That summer before we separated, I went on holiday with my parents and my daughter, and I floated just above depression. Or, rather, it floated just above me, ready to consume. Everything felt like an effort, everything my parents did annoyed me. I behaved like a surly teenager, barely washing a dish, grumbling and arguing with my mother constantly.

Unsticking myself from the leather couch wasn't hard just because of the heat. I was exhausted.

We got home, and I lay on another couch, alone in my living room. Peeling myself off still felt like an effort beyond my capabilities.

There is an invisible cloud that hovers above all of us but now I had my own personal cloud. I felt it so viscerally I could almost see it. A huge, grey cloud. Long and rectangular – almost like a mattress. Puffy. It hovered above me and I realised immediately what it was there to do. It was there to engulf me.

I know what this is, I thought. *This is a kind of depression.* I knew that, if I allowed it, it would drag me under. Offering a sort of reprieve from it all (temporary, obviously, for there is nothing of the gently sedative about depression). For a minute, it was deceptively seductive. A going under, a sort of inverted, dark-side coping mechanism for when it all gets too much.

Months later, when I interview Elizabeth Gilbert for my podcast, she describes this kind of depression. A repressing of all the stuff that was too hard to face.

I saw it coming for me. A black dog. A wave that threatened to capsize all in its path.

It was the thought of my daughter that kick-started my return. Allowed me to find, somewhere deep within, a spur. I realised that staying still and not facing the fact that something was terribly wrong would mean going under.

My feet touched the bottom but they kicked back, pushing me up towards the surface. *I must*, I thought, *or I will go under. If it is a choice between an ending or going under, then let the marriage end.*

Anger feels like one step above depression. Hovering over it. Depression is an umbrella term, a psychologist tells me, there are as many types really as there are minds. In some cases, it is caused when a person forces their emotions down. Flatlines them.

At least with anger, there is energy. And, so, I have rage days, as I come to call them. Sometimes, they are almost enjoyable, those anger days. Easier than the grief days, which are heavy and so, so tiring. With grief, you cannot imagine having the stamina to do normal things ever again. At least anger is an energy. You can turn that energy into fuel.

Not a dead-end after all, as it happens.

And when the white heat of your anger burns off, you might find that it is useful in putting up boundaries where before there were none.

'I'm not angry,' I tell Helen again one day. A few minutes later I tell her how I've had enough of a particular situation. 'I'm not accepting it anymore.'

'That's anger, Lia,' she laughs and shakes her head at my ongoing reluctance to be an angry woman.

'OK,' I say, admitting to a defeat of kinds. 'I'm angry.'

I had never thought too much about how emotions could be scary. The fear that they might capsize you. You have to hope that you have the right amount of resilience to return to equilibrium. Or the right sort of navigation.

A sort of emotional equation: grief plus anger divided by resilience plus navigator = return to emotional wellbeing.

Part Two

Picking up the Pieces

Chapter 14

How to Be Alone. How to Be Lonely.

Saturday evenings are the worst. The first one after my husband has moved out, I am taken by surprise by the loneliness.

I am caught unawares, without a plan with which to defeat or protect myself from it.

My father has been here for the afternoon, helping with the completion of a child's IKEA kitchen (fully taking over while I sat exhausted on the floor watching, pretending to be deeply involved in reading the instructions that, given it is IKEA, are a handful of images which take seconds to look through). It had been a Christmas present the year before but had remained only half completed. The top half, that bit with the built-in microwave, had been a victim of things falling apart. That had been a Christmas of getting by, of doing the minimum, all efforts focused on the last bit of holding things together.

What reserves we had left had been exhausted by the putting together of the main body of the thing. The top half of our daughter's Scandi kitchen had defeated us, left in its box in the hall, an innocent bystander caught up in events, collateral damage of a marriage disintegrating.

Around 4 o'clock, my father begins gathering his things to go. Bedtime still seems like hours away, hours for which I have nothing planned. *We're not ready for idle time* I think, beginning to panic. I cannot ask him to stay, a man who has spent his afternoon wrestling with plywood, tolerating the 'help' of a three-year-old, only to find, crushingly, at the end of it all, that we have forgotten to include the damn bar for the pot hooks. His couch and the rugby match are calling him.

It's too late to ring anyone – plans will have been made – and I don't really want the effort of socialising anyhow. And I have a child to feed and put to bed. After a long, tiring week, I do not want to entertain. I want to be settling down with the other adult who lives in my house, except now there is no other adult. This is the tricky spot in getting used to living on your own. Becoming comfortable being alone in the times when you don't want to entertain but are not busy doing things.

My father leaves, and I decide at five o'clock, dinner time, that we should go for a walk. I panic, basically.

It's a disastrously ill-judged idea, but I can't face sitting around.

We drive to our local village and set out on our walk; an exact triangle taking in the strip of local shops – that, to my overly sensitive eyes, are full of parents picking up last-minute bits with which to fuel the evening of family time ahead – a grim stretch of terrace and a quiet, deserted grey concrete lane that I would normally never contemplate walking down.

It is clear immediately that the walk was a mistake, but I refuse to give up. We are going for the walk, depressing as it is.

Afterwards, at home, and after my daughter is in bed, I find a piece by the journalist Sali Hughes, in which she describes how a slow dread of Saturday nights set in after her divorce. (I am, at this time, undergoing an attempt to read the entire internet on the aftermath of separation and divorce.)

My favourite are first-person accounts from those who have gone before me.

Sali describes the setting in and deepening of the loneliness on a Saturday night, at home with two small children. How it could feel like the rest of the world was either steeped in domestic (for which, read 'two adults') bliss or out having the absolute time of their lives.

So, she instigated movie night. Instead of stewing in her own sense of aloneness, every Saturday night, she and her two small boys would climb into bed with pizzas and popcorn and watch a movie. I hold her message close: it will get better. This too shall pass.

Chapter 15

Connect Four

Everyone needs connection to others.

My brother and I were raised as non-religious. First generation Irish non-Catholics, to distinguish from lapsed Catholics. We were never one, then the other; we have never been religious. Our parents were both brought up as Catholics and then decided against it. 'Lapsed' is the wrong word in their case, suggesting as it does a passive slide with the occasional visit to mass at Christmas.

Theirs was a fully punctuated walking away.

Along with friends, my parents set up the third multi-denominational primary school in the country, one aim being that we wouldn't have to leave the classroom during religious education. It also meant that we had a purpose-built community of other non-religious types, something you take for granted when you grow up in the middle of it, but, looking back, something that was hugely helpful. Today, Educate Together schools are common in Ireland, but they weren't when I was a child. Being non-religious was to be different, not always something small children relish.

So there was our family of four non-religious types. But, more than that, we were surrounded by people who thought nothing of our choice, rather than find it something slightly startling, which it still was in 1980s Ireland.

When you are not religious, you come to realise that a lot of people who are work from a default setting that assumes that you are in some way lacking. You are not. You create your own airbag. Find your own people, support network and rituals. Your sense of being linked in. Everyone needs a connection to others. Never more so than when your biggest connection comes asunder.

Chapter 16

The Woman in the Mirror

A month after we separated, my old college friend Pam came from London where she now lives, to visit with her daughter who is a year older than mine. In college, Pam was the person who held others together, or at least stopped them from going over the edge. Long before she had a daughter, she was mothering everyone around her.

Her stamina has always been legendary. Years before she was a single mother living in London with no family nearby and a huge job, she was the I-don't-know-how-she-does-it woman. Only, back then, in college, we wondered at how she could hold down an almost full-time shift job, her college workload, a huge network of friends and party harder than anyone.

Pam knew everyone and she knew them properly, not just politely.

It's been several years since we have caught up properly but that doesn't matter. Pam is the kind of person to whom you can unburden your most troubling secrets within minutes of reuniting after years of absence from each other's lives. She will not flinch, no matter how strange, dark and disturbing you might care to make it, she will merely go into managing, helping, commiserating and supporting mode. And she's funny as hell.

Despite this, that day in Dublin, we spend two of our three hours together making what I later realise was essentially polite small talk, given what I by then knew was going on below the surface for both of us.

We were skirmishing.

And then one of us said something, and the other realised that there was more to it, and we recognised something in each other. And suddenly it all came spilling out. The children were parked in front of Peppa and given ice-creams to ensure no interruptions, as we crammed it all into that last hour before they had to leave.

It turned out we are in exactly the same situation. Both our marriages had fallen apart under similar circumstances.

Like me, she had barely told anyone yet and was only in the first few months. We told each other everything.

She too has a small child, a little girl. We reflected each other exactly, in our recent past and present.

After she goes home to London, we text, sometimes regularly, sometimes out of the blue after weeks of silence. Whatever the time gap, these texts cut right to the heart of matters; no polite preamble is needed. Out of nowhere: 'How are you? How is she?'

Finding Pam makes me realise how much I need to find other women in the same boat.

Chapter 17

The First Wives Club

The grief of a relationship ending and early motherhood have a surprising amount in common. The physicality of it; exhaustion unlike any tiredness you've ever known. The roller-coaster of never knowing how you will feel from one moment to the next, and the wear-you-downness of having no control over that.

Right *now* you're fine, but you can sense the upset, hovering above you like a barrel that keeps filling with water, ready to spill and overwhelm you at any minute. You just don't know exactly when it will fall.

You will sometimes hear a woman say that, when she became a mother, she grieved the loss of her former self. Becoming separated is similar, except you grieve the loss of your imagined future self. The life you had expected to live, even if this is only in the broadest of brush strokes.

Both letting go of your partner in life and becoming a mother have the ability to render you emotionally raw – more raw than you have ever been in your entire life.

And in both, at the start, are so many moments that, while you're in them, feel like this is it, this is my life now. This will never change. The baby will never sleep for more than two hours. I will never not feel heartbroken that my daughter and her father live under different roofs. And then you look back and see it was a phase and that it has passed without you even realising.

Like early motherhood, to cope with the sense of loss at the beginning of a separation I need other people who know exactly how I am feeling. What I am dealing with. People to whom I do not need to explain because, having experienced it, they can see it from the inside out.

People who won't say that they understand what I'm going through because their husbands are away working all the time. I know this is well meaning, and it actually doesn't bother me at all, but neither does it help me. I need women who actually, really do get it.

I had known my friend Ruth for years through work. She is separated with one child, though she is much farther down the road than me. We meet once or twice a year on a job and afterwards always say that we should go for coffee. We both know we want to, but also that we are unlikely to. Busyness, rather than lack of interest.

Now, in the aftermath of the separation, I text her and ask if we can, finally, go for the coffee. I suggest the Westbury Hotel because if you are going to get together to discuss the demise of your marriage and how you will cope with said demise, then you go where they have the best coffee and scones you can think of.

Once, as we sat chatting when the tape had been turned off after I had interviewed her for a *Sunday Independent* article on mothering and working, I asked Ruth what it was like to be a single parent. How hard was it. 'Actually,' she said, 'sometimes it's easier to do it yourself.' She didn't mean this as a reflection on her ex, but rather the fact that when a marriage has gone bad, it is easier for both parents to parent out of range of each other, rather than together.

Now, I realise I need more of this kind of thinking. This glimmer that things will be OK.

Theodore Roosevelt once said that 'comparison is the thief of joy'. However, comparing similarities between your life and someone else's, rather than differences, can be the source of it.

I need women who have experienced exactly this sense of loss for a future that looked a certain way and a present that has fallen apart. I need them because they know that this is not an unbearable tragedy. They won't look at me in ill-concealed horror. Won't subject me to the *sad-for-you* head tilt.

Being a journalist enables me to have a certain level of nosiness. Encourages it, really. Asking questions about people's lives for a living allows for a lack of conversational barriers.

You get beyond small talk fairly speedily. It means I have ready access to a wide circle of women who I know through work.

I become able to spot them; women who, like me, are just about holding themselves together. Their outside-world self, tightly wound and brittle smile pasted over the cracked, blurry, grief-stricken self that hovers just below the surface.

Ruth has been through it, and so she is a comfort in the present for being a messenger from the future. When she says, 'Things will be OK – you will get through this', I believe her. She proves this truth by her very existence. The words carry more weight coming from her, because she really shows it to be true.

She is the first member of what I come to think of as my First Wives Club – women I collect to myself, some I've known for years, others I've met since the separation. Initially, they are women who, like me, were once married and now are not. Then, the club expands to include women who have dealt with other things. They are First Wives because the first plan didn't work out. Now, they are on their second life plan, or beyond.

Eventually, my First Wives are any woman whose life has strayed from the accepted traditional path, the received notion of what a woman's life should look like to be deemed a success.

Some are women who have had to create a new normal. An alternate to that which they might have hoped for themselves. So, there are the women who have separated, but also women whose husbands are ill, women who never married, who never had children, or who lost a child. Some of these losses are greater than others, of course. Some are not losses but choices. This is not a competitive sport.

What all these women have in common is that they fell outside the traditional, whether by choice or by circumstance.

I meet Ruth for coffee and our conversation is all finishing each other's sentences – 'I knows' and 'Oh God me toos'. 'Did you do this?' 'Feel this?' We laugh together, as you only can with people who get it from the absolute inside. Who are not embarrassed or scared by your grief and don't feel the need to tread cautiously on eggshells around it.

We walk slowly to the car park. It's a warm autumn day and we hold our coats over our arms, no need for them. We stand beside my car chatting, reluctant to say goodbye. I walk away feeling better than I have in weeks.

Chapter 18

How Do You Solve a Problem? Ask Maria

You cannot do it on your own, this finding your way back out, or through. With depression, you may need medication to help you get there.

'First-line treatment', it's called. Which, in my head, becomes 'front line'. The front line of defence. That little leg up that enables you to start contemplating taking on a problem. That bit of leverage.

I am not depressed but I am precariously close to overwhelm. aria is my front line in teaching me the skills with which to confront this. She is a life coach, and I first meet her when we do a ten-week one-to-one assertiveness course together, several years before my marriage ended. Now, she is also my friend, worn down by my relentless campaign of suggesting coffees and walks along the coastline where she lives.

My editor had run a feature where, over a number of weeks, several journalists would learn a new skill. Being asked to pitch for it felt like the adult equivalent of being given free rein in a sweetshop. Like making a superhuman version of myself. Or at the very least, a slightly new and improved one.

What new skill would I choose to acquire?

My mother had done an assertiveness course with her sister in the 1970s and had always talked about it in such glowing terms that I had been left with a longstanding wish to do one of my own. The broken-record approach was her big takeaway and became a major part of her parenting arsenal. I wore down many a primary-school nemesis with a very basic version of it, simply repeating the same sentence over and over again, as we had practised at bedtime the night before.

After my editor accepts my pitch, a quick search online unearths Maria. All the other life coaches I come across give off a stridency that suggests I might need an assertiveness course just to contemplate dealing with them in the first place. In contrast, Maria's beaming smile leapt off the screen on her website's home page.

I ring and leave a message, explaining my suggested project. She teaches me assertiveness, and I write about it. I am on a job when she calls, and I sneak off to take her call. 'I will work with you, Lia.' She is Chilean, with a warmth that flows down through the phone.

In person, she greets me, always, with arms open, and a cry of 'Lia, my beautiful friend'.

Assertiveness seemed like a good skill to practise. When we met, I was embarking on a freelance career, having given up a staff newspaper job so I could spend more time with my daughter.

In retrospect, it wasn't a bad skill to have if you are forced to confront the fact that your life is falling apart. Maybe it is the skill that will leverage you into a place where you are able to face the fact that it has already fallen apart. Cut through the bullshit (you are telling yourself, if nothing else), and face the truth.

'Assertiveness is a skill of communication,' Maria explains. 'A way to communicate within conflict. It is logical. Take out the emotion. Knowing what you want is crucial. You can't be assertive without it.'

Now, at this moment, I haven't a clue what I want. Even if I did, it feels like it wouldn't matter, things have got so far beyond any sense of having control. But Maria is full of life skills, which she teaches me as we walk up and down the harbour walls. She calms the fear, makes me think I can brave this out. This feels like a place to start. Or at least, a ledge to stand on, to stop the freefall.

Chapter 19

A Home to Work From

After we were married, but before I was pregnant, an older male colleague said to me (it's always the older, white men with their unwanted reflections on one's life), 'Sure you'll go off now, have a baby and disappear.'

'Oh God, no,' I replied instantly, almost as a reflex, without really considering what I *actually* thought, or wanted. 'If I *do* have a baby, I'll be back within six months, maximum.'

I knew by then that I *did* want to have a baby. But it seemed important to assert that becoming a mother would in no way effect my dedication to my work.

A small part of my reaction was to do with the fact that I had worked hard to carve out a niche for myself in my dream job, working in the fashion-and-features sections of a national newspaper. Ever since the day RTÉ's Charlie Bird had come to our classroom for careers week in primary school and told us with great relish about his job, I had wanted to be a journalist.

There is nowhere as fun to work as in a newsroom, and nobody as fun to work with as journalists.

They are opinionated, irreverent, able to talk to you about everything from celebrity doings to the latest book you *need* to read, often (although not always) highly intelligent, gossipy, bitchy – the most fun.

I worked in an office run largely by two women, both of whom had juggled work and motherhood, and who vociferously supported other younger women in doing so. Even still, talking to this older man, acknowledging the desire to make room in my life for motherhood, rather than shunting it into the spaces between work – snatches of weekday mornings and evenings, and crammed full weekends – felt like something I should not admit to. The idea that I might want to change things around to make room for motherhood, instinctively felt like something that should be denied.

And then the end of maternity leave approached, and I felt a grey, heavy feeling settle over me. It pressed down upon me and, no matter how I tried, I could not get out from underneath it, it held me in its grip, a large, smothering duvet of a cloud. 'That's grief,' a friend said immediately when I described how I was feeling, and my many failed attempts to make myself feel better about the prospect of leaving my daughter to go back to five days a week in the office. 'You're grieving.'

She had recently lost her mother, so knew about these things. About the relentless, will-not-be-ignored nature of grief. How it holds you in stasis, the awful knowledge that some days there is nothing you can do to make this go away, to make yourself feel better. That you must simply push through the bad days, tell yourself this will pass. 'Push through' is probably too energised a phrase really. Sit through is more like it – wade, at best.

Although on this occasion I could not see how it would pass. I returned to work and things got worse. A colleague would ask casually how my daughter was getting on, and I would have to run to the bathrooms, barely making it to a cubicle before I started crying.

Lots of other people manage this return to work, stop being such a drama queen, I berated myself, frustrated by my own upset. *You've worked for years to create this role. What is wrong with you? Stop this. Get on with it.*

But I couldn't. And so, after several months, I left and went freelance in order to spend as much time with my daughter as possible. Being flexible seemed essential after I became a mother. As it turned out, it was an absolute non-negotiable when I became a single parent.

I work from home now. We call it my floating office,

my daughter and I, because I move from dining room table, to desk, to sitting on the couch, to occasionally sitting on my bed.

A child anchors you in the home. They render the pay-offs of domestic life more enjoyable. The creation of a cosy home. A home-cooked meal. Ironically, it is these totems of family life that support us after the break up. I enjoy the duties and chores of a traditional wife more than ever now that I am no longer a wife. Being a homemaker seems all the more important.

In the weeks after her birth, I realised that she could manage one day out and about, full of stimulation and ignoring her nap schedules, but that this overstimulation needed to be followed by a quiet day spent ticking away in the routine and refuge of home, just the two of us.

Now that it *is* just the two of us living here, I realise again that it is important to lean in to that quiet refuge. To not always be running out the door to fill the spaces. To brave the empty Sunday afternoons. To be able to sit in the quiet of our own home, us two, and for that to feel OK. Not bereft, or lonely, or like something is missing. For us two to be enough.

For anyone newly facing into this, this is not something you will become comfortable with overnight. And before you get truly comfortable with it, you will think you are, and then be taken by surprise again by feeling jarred by it.

I had wanted flexibility with my work to spend time with her. Not to work less, just on a different timescale. Now, as a single parent, both flexibility and not working less take on a different importance. And, of course, working from home.

After the separation, only having to get one of us outside-world-appropriate before the playschool run is a small luxury that helps hugely. I buy a long, quilted coat from Penneys, which is tantamount to wearing a duvet, and on especially exhausted days, swap pyjama bottoms for leggings, but leave the rest as it was when I rolled out of bed, sometimes not even bothering to put a bra on, retreating immediately to the house after I've dropped my daughter to school.

This uniform encases me – low maintenance, easily adopted comforting armour for leaving home.

As a newly single parent, working from home feels like an essential part of our recovery plan. A non-negotiable. I need to be here. To tend to our home. To tether this place that will ground us throughout. Become our safe space.

I know logically that it won't, but I feel that, if I were to leave every day for an office, this home, which I am so carefully trying to reconstruct, might crumble and disappear entirely. I am keeping the home fires burning (not literally, we have two chimneys, but the life admin involved in finding a chimney sweep overwhelms me).

Dark, cosy bedrooms with a warm, tiny daughter

to cuddle into. Our L-shaped couch upon which to lounge for movies, endless movies; on my own, with my daughter, my friends, my brother.

Bedrooms to be tidied; the putting away of stuff and subsequent creation of calm which that bestows, the sense of smoothing things down offering a sense of control that has been so lacking. Hours spent pottering. My daughter in the bath while I weave in and out, tidying. Upstairs, she plays with her dolls, jumps on her bed while I go in and out of the two bedrooms, putting away laundry.

This isn't to suggest a picture of only domestic bliss. Obviously, having a home is a privilege. But running one on your own as a single parent can feel relentless.

For a time after he moves out, I am on high alert for any encroachments on the boundaries of our patch. Hyper-vigilantly defending our territory. New neighbours move in and park their car outside our house for several days, an infringement of personal space previously not countenanced on our terrace of seven.

'There are no houses opposite and there is ample parking. What are they thinking?' I wail to my brother, outraged. He tries to muster a look of sympathy.

For a week I hover at the window, waiting to spot them leaving the house. 'Miss Marple, is it? my family say at the sight of me peering from behind a blind. ITV afternoon TV is my happy place, anything preceded by an ad for a reclining chair or a leisurely river cruise.

I twitch at the curtains, hoping to dash out and stage a casual 'bumping into' when they leave the house, where I will politely but firmly ask them to move the car. Half of me knows this behaviour is mad, the other half cannot *bear* to have this car sitting outside our house, in our spot.

I need them to get off my territory. Meant in the politest possible way you understand. You are new, but this is our home, our place of recovery. Be mindful of our boundaries. Do not trespass upon them.

Chapter 20

Bra off/Pyjamas on, People

'Oh, we're having a slumber party, are we?' Soph says briskly, taking me in as I opened the front door. It was movie night and I was already in my pyjamas; bra off, slippers on.

Making the decision to end a marriage is the earthquake. The endless small changes you must then accommodate in your life, some not imagined until you come right up against them, are the aftershocks.

The consequences and realities that were part of that original decision which you don't think about until they occur. Living without another adult is a big one. Of course, you knew that was a consequence. But you know it in the abstract. Then you begin to live alone, and you see that you need your People Without Preamble, as I come to think of them.

People whose presence in my house is as easy as if they lived there.

I find them, and I create habitual social routines with them. It helps to ease gently into the new way.

Sophie and I do a regular movie night. My father comes for Wednesday-night roasts. My mother puts my daughter to bed Thursdays while I work, and stays on for tea and chats afterwards.

My neighbour's grandson spends several afternoons a week next door with his grandmother. 'Want to come for a playdate?' my daughter shouts at him over the garden wall. He arrives at the door proudly proffering a toy.

His mother is also separated; we become friends. 'I got loads done while they were playing,' I tell her when she comes to collect him.

'Enjoy it while they're occupied,' she replies. 'Sit on the couch, read your book. Do nothing.'

She understands the raising of an only child, and the demands for play that this can involve. The need, as a single parent, any parent really, to snatch your breaks as and when they appear.

Chapter 21
Movie Night

In Sali Hughes's piece about the at-home movie nights she began with her sons following her divorce, she adds that now, years later and remarried, she wouldn't consider leaving the house on a Saturday night. Not only had she insulated herself against the loneliness until the loneliness had gone away, she had created a tradition.

This is key to building the new way, I realise. Creating traditions upon which to hang your new life. They become the scaffolding, without which you will flounder.

Soon after my husband moves out, after that first disastrous, lonely Saturday, I plan a movie night. The discussion about which movie we will watch goes on all week. We haven't seen *Moana*, and my daughter grudgingly agrees to a break from *Frozen*, *The Bee Movie* and *Shrek 2*, our usual oeuvres. Excited, we get into bed at half-past four – we cannot wait any longer. We have our starter; popcorn and a margherita pizza. Earlier, we had walked around the corner to our local shop for treats – jellies.

It changes everything, movie night. We barely notice the arrival of bedtime, wish it away so we can watch the film until the end, rather than (me) counting the minutes.

The next Saturday, my father and brother join us for movie night, having heard of the week before's fun. *Moana* again (and for the foreseeable future, obviously, my daughter having a small-child's tolerance for watching a favourite movie into the ground). All three adults squish into my bed eating pizza, my daughter in the middle, a hand reaching up to my ear fiddling unconsciously, a leg flung over Grandad.

Chapter 22

Running on Nothing

It's almost impossible to talk about self-care nowadays, so self-parodic has it become. That doesn't make it redundant. In the immediate aftermath of a crisis, self-care looks almost invisible – more what you don't do, than what you do.

This is ground zero, and I am using every last ounce of mental and physical energy I have just to keep going. To meet work deadlines, feed myself and my child, stay on top of the parts of life admin that simply cannot be allowed to slide, and procrastinate about the parts that can so that they join my list of things to worry about at four in the morning.

'Running on nothing but adrenaline,' a friend who is going through something similar says months later.

A to-do list of things intended to make me feel better would just become something to feel bad about not doing.

So, right at the start, I don't go to the gym. I don't meditate or do yoga or even go for walks. The thought of setting the immersion on time, filling the tub, then getting in and out and all the faff around having a bath – because even the nice things feel like a list of chores when everything around you is crashing down – is exhausting.

Mostly, I am just glad to make it to the couch after my daughter's bedtime.

There is little room for anything but 'getting through'. There is no space, or energy, for things like having some friends over for dinner, going for a run or even committing to a new Netflix series.

I make my life small; that is all I can manage. 'We retreated into a bunker,' my friend Georgie tells me of when she was unwell.

I'm in my bunker. My safety zone. It's only when I leave it, and then return, exhausted by the outside world, that I am even aware of its existence. I move between a small number of specific places – my own home, my parents' house, the gym (where Sophie and I work together in the reception), and her house for afternoon playdates and weekend breakfasts; the kids playing around us, Sophie and I providing them with snacks while we sit drinking coffee.

I find anything or anyone outside the points on this safety grid exhausting, and to be avoided when at all possible. The pretence of being OK is too taxing.

When I wake in the mornings there is a moment of peace – and then I would remember, then it would hit me all over again; a clunk of nausea, in my throat and in my belly. I would try to shrug it off, but the feeling had to be carried around all day, both a sinking from below and a pushing down from above, an invisible yoke, pulling at me from all directions, a weight I could not get away from, dragging behind, above, around me.

So self-care, in the middle of this, was simply a matter of stopping.

I stopped drinking. This wasn't the grand gesture it might have been for someone else. I am too lightweight a drinker to ever have been much of one, more likely to fall asleep after a couple of glasses than make serious inroads into any bottle. But any drinking I did left me feeling angry the next day. And tired. And parenting alone with a hangover is dreadful – the few drinks are simply not worth it. Adding to the already cumbersome, exhausting burden I was already carrying just didn't make sense.

I stopped to give myself every chance of feeling as good as I possibly could, given the circumstances. To look after myself.

Self-care, the invisible kind.

I stopped looking at Instagram on weekend evenings,

in order to save myself from falling down a well of feeling sad at how everyone else's life compared to mine.

I took to eating Bounty Bars with a vengeance.

In the grand scheme of great overindulgences, I am aware that a second Bounty Bar with a cup of tea every evening, sat on my couch after my daughter was asleep, isn't up there with the greats. But I began to feel like I was overdoing it.

'I need to eat more healthily,' I sigh to my mother, who responds with a barely concealed eye-roll and a witheringly delivered retort that food is there to comfort us.

In-the-thick-of-it self-care can be just a matter of stopping doing the things that inhibit or threaten your sense of wellbeing. Or simply doing things that might not fall within the canon of Instagram influencer-approved self-care, but that just make you feel better, right in that moment.

Things like eating the second Bounty Bar or lying in bed all day when you have childcare, and not bothering to do the friends, walks, gym stuff all the lists say will help.

I am the swan, apparently serene (or so I would tell myself), gliding above all frantic paddling. Everything I could muster was going into simply getting through the day. So I took my comfort where I could. An extra Bounty with my cup of tea on the couch wasn't hurting anyone.

Chapter 23

The Work Wife Who Became a Sister-Wife

Slowly, in almost invisible increments, I moved from the static to the kinetic. I was ready for action, of sorts. Ready to start putting together a sort of scaffolding around this new life that I was attempting to build. Things that would both prop me up and strengthen me to do more. To go forward, move out of the bomb site, clear out the rubble and rebuild.

To our own surprise as much as that of anyone else, Sophie and I became people who had gurus.

This is not us. We are the type of people who laugh up our sleeves at such things. Who roll our eyes at inspirational quotations. Scoff at the very notion of healers.

I first met Sophie when we were set up on a shopping trip.

I was working as a stylist, and people were always imagining that I would be only too delighted to spend further time in the shops in my spare time, helping them to shop. But this expedition was different to anything either of us had previously attempted. We were both pregnant and shopping for baby paraphernalia, that first meeting was to buy supplies for her hospital bag.

Sophie was pregnant with her first child, Roo, who became a beautiful long-lashed boy, a painter like his mother, and my daughter's first friend. Together they now form a dream playdate team who will entertain each other for hours while we sit downstairs and chat. He calls her 'my darling'. After playschool one day, my daughter showed me one of those photocopied pictures they colour in. 'My family' was written above a picture of three children. 'It's me, Roo and Ari,' she said. Sophie's boys.

'Love you Sary.' 'Love you Roo', they sometimes shout after each other as we leave a playdate. They're often mistaken for siblings when we're out and about; a physical match for each other as well as a temperamental one.

Amongst the many press shopping discount cards I had been sent as a journalist who wrote about fashion, was a card with a very generous discount for Mothercare. Of little interest before, now both of us were pregnant – me twelve weeks, Sophie about to give birth – we found ourselves on a shopping date arranged by my editor, her mother.

She arrived wearing a tartan coat and a lilac jumper which immediately made me rethink my previous feelings on a colour I had until then always deemed drab. Sophie looks like someone from a Wes Anderson movie most of the time. She has naturally almost white-blonde hair, which falls in enviable beach waves when she lets it dry naturally, alabaster skin and is generally to be found wearing bright-red lipstick. She and her mother share a bafflement at anyone who does not wear lipstick. Preparing together for a night out, she once silently handed me a MAC lipstick pallet. Brand new. 'Take it,' she insisted. 'I don't want it, it was a gift. Not my colours.' I think she couldn't handle the sight of my faintly lip-balmed mouth any longer.

Within minutes of meeting, we were deep in discussion over exactly what size pads she would need after the baby was born. This is very on-brand for Soph, a person with whom no topic is off limits. Unshockable (unless you're gossiping, in which case she can greet a titbit with exactly the kind of delighted, intrigued, dramatic relish you require) her own honesty is untrammelled.

'She's *so* honest', people always say to me about her writing. Or is it just that the rest of us are so dissembling?

It is impossible to be a woman now and not, to some extent, be performing your own version of the notion of womanhood imposed upon us all. We cannot simply be, we women, we must be a *kind* of eating, a *kind* of looking, a *kind* of mothering, or not mothering. A career woman, or not. We are all takes on a version of femininity that has been imposed on us from outside. Womanhood is a conscious performance.

I think that if we feel threatened by another woman, it is often because we feel she is making a better job at it than we are. We're in a sort of horrible competition with each other we never asked to take part in.

Instagram didn't do that. The patriarchal society we live in did, long before social media was invented.

More than anyone I know, Sophie performs being a woman in a way that is truest to her real self. And she makes it look more fun than most. As it happens, these are excellent qualities to have in a friend who is going to help you to create a new self, a new life, when you have to go out in the world again on your own.

When your marriage ends, you need people who are fun, because the fun dies first, and it can be the slowest thing to come back. You can't force it; when life is all about coping and getting through and the anxiety of it all, fun disappears.

After Sophie had her baby, I was sitting in the office beside her mother, also a woman to be relied upon for sheer honesty. Each week she would hiss at me, 'The first two weeks are a nightmare. A *night*-mare.' It went on to become the first four weeks, six, eight.

Happily ensconced in my princess pregnancy (smug af in other words), blind to what was to come, I blithely ignored her. *Clearly, Sophie isn't reading the right books*, I thought with a pomposity that was punished within months by a child who refused to sleep for more than two hours for much of her first six months. *I have Gina Ford and I shall be fine*, I thought to myself, rereading the schedules listed in the book yet again.

Except of course, Sophie's mother was right. A baby is a joy, but they are also a car crash into your life. My daughter was a reflux baby, refusing to sleep without hours of rocking. A week in, a broken shell, crashing after the high of the birth and the excitement of her arrival, her words came back to me.

I clung to them like a woman on the verge of drowning. It was not just me. At least one other person had found this as hard. And if one other had, then probably lots had. I was not the only one to have felt like she was utterly failing in the face of a newborn.

Even better than her mother's words, Sophie herself arrived at the house, one of the first people to visit. None of her friends had yet had babies, and she later told me she was determined to forge a friendship with me, which we did, despite potential deal breakers – that I will happily drink instant coffee over plunger, refrigerate eggs and borrow and not return her Tupperware.

On that first visit, she brought a breastfeeding cushion, a receptacle for the baby that unlike all the others we had purchased which were then still too big, she didn't slide out of when I tried to have a shower or just put her down for even five minutes, that night's dinner and cake. All subsequent guests were judged harshly against the standard she set.

She took one look at me, hair bedraggled, formerly baby-blue dressing gown now greying, covered in milk stains but too tired to even care about making an effort in front of her, and announced briskly, 'You're in the hole.' It was said in the tone of someone to whom this was not out of the ordinary, a fact that was, in itself, deeply reassuring. Another friend had done the same for her shortly after Roo had been born, diagnosing a low point she had felt but hadn't admitted even to herself. This is happening, it is normal, it is will pass. Knowledge passed from woman to woman like a gift.

She named the hole, and then she helped me out of it.

Now, I am again in the hole. Actually we both are. It is a bad year for us both. I lose my marriage, Sophie loses her father.

As my relationship with my husband disappeared, she had been losing her lovely father to Alzheimer's. They are very different types of loss, but Sophie understands what it is to lose a person, to lose the relationship you had with them, even though they are still right there in front of you. To look at someone once-beloved and feel none of the love you once thought was guaranteed from them.

We are in the hole, but at least we are in it together.

Grief days sometimes feel like moving through resistance. As if you're so weighed down that even the smallest task feels daunting. Having Sophie means having someone to get through those days with, someone who simply gets it, who doesn't need explanations, or for whom some kind of front needs to be put on, because she is right there too.

Sometimes, you can show how you feel to your friends in a way you cannot to your family because you know those feelings may upset your parent or a sibling in a way they wouldn't a friend. They're more able to bear the sight of it. Friends can provide a place that feels safe for you to fall apart – however temporarily – and then get back up again and keep going. They also replace a spouse in a way family can't, for the simple fact of being about the same age as you. You are experiencing life's joys and challenges at roughly the same time. That is a safety net in itself, when you lose the person you thought you would grow old with. Now, I plan future weekends away in retirement with Sophie and Rachel and Shereen.

At the start of grief, a lot of it is just about waiting it out. You can't rush it or force it to pass, you simply need to count off the days. Get through. With Sophie, I had someone to do that with. To slump in the soft play area of our gym with. Sit outside classes waiting for our children, chatting idly. Go to the park at the weekend. Someone to distract the children when it got too much and I would cry, sitting in the middle of McDonalds. It makes all the difference.

'I don't remember that?' Shereen says to me one day much later, when we sit on the couch in her sister's large kitchen, discussing part of this book. There's a worried frown between her eyebrows. I'm describing a difficult time, and she looks at me blankly. 'I didn't know about that,' she says.

The thing is, in the midst, there is only time and energy for one day-to-day, moment-to-moment, person. In the first flush of grief, you make your world small. Sophie was the one person who knew the minutiae. The person who knew my entire world.

Chapter 24

A-OK

'It always makes me *so* sad,' a friend said, 'to see families where there are children, and the marriage has ended. Because I know that that things will never really be OK again.'

It was after we had decided to end the marriage but before we had told everyone.

I stopped breathing for a moment, my brain felt as if it had clenched inside my skull, like something had kicked my innards. It wasn't her fault; she didn't know that we were in the process of separating.

Much later, I find out that this friend's marriage had, in fact, been going through a dangerously rough patch at the time. Teetering on the brink. When she said this, she was staring into the abyss; the mouth of roaring terror that opens up when you contemplate your main relationship being over, and everything needing to be ripped up.

Much later, I realise that she spoke out of her own fear.

She doesn't notice me freeze, and I say nothing, let it slide. Self-consciously rearrange the items on the sill of the window we are standing by, murmur a noncommittal, 'Mmmhhhmmmm'.

But, in my head, I am shouting 'no', fists clenched, foot stamping. Because even then, right in the middle of everything falling apart, I knew that what she said wasn't true. That this was not a situation where things would never be alright again.

For one thing, I knew that I simply would not let that be the case. There was no way that, at this early stage of life, my daughter and I were going to be written off as not OK, indefinitely. *For Christ's sake, no one has even died,* I wanted to shout. *Everyone is getting out of this alive.*

Intentions aside, whether or not I would allow it, I also just knew that that we would be OK. That this was a sad event, and a stressful, exhausting, angering time, but that we would get through it, and that everything would be good again.

Of course, this was not the optimum outcome. Not what we would have chosen. But who gets a life that is in all senses what they have chosen? If that's the criterion, then frankly none of us are going to be alright.

Besides, I'm raising my daughter to believe that it's fine not to be OK sometimes.

Chapter 25

The Wellness Plan

Grief does funny things to a person. It breaks you in lots of small, ongoing ways. Hairline fractures. Putting yourself back together isn't just one big push to move on. You need lots of little things to bolster you. To help you through the bad days.

Before you put yourself back together, you must just keep yourself from falling apart again and again.

Which is why Sophie and I now find ourselves over our breakfast phone call (our freelancers-working-from-home version of the making-tea-in-the-office-kitchen morning chat), having polite, just shy of passive aggressive, conversations in which we attempt to one up each other over our chosen life coaches.

Mine is Maria. Hers is Judith, a woman I will later shoehorn my way in on.

'Judith is just *such* a wonderful mixture of the practical *and the emotional*,' Sophie says.

'Yes yes, of course that is what *I* have loved about Maria for *months* now,' I reply grimly.

Maria ('my- friend-the-life-coach', as she becomes known when I quote her endlessly to family and friends) is high energy in the best possible way. Not the draining, full-of-edgy-pent-upness kind that leaves you feeling slightly on edge yourself, as if you've drunk too much coffee. But the kind where you come away feeling as if you are a smartphone that has been plugged into its charger.

Re-energised.

'How do you do it?' I ask her one day as we're sitting in her back garden, moving every half hour to follow the sun patch. 'Always stay so full of energy, when you pump so much of it into other people?' It must take so much out of her, I think, knowing how restored I always feel when I leave her.

'Oh, I have a wellness plan,' she says casually, as if this was the most obvious thing in the world.

A *what?*

Whatever it is, I want one.

Maria explains. A wellness plan is a variety of habits you incorporate into your life that will help to keep you on the emotional straight and narrow. Mentally buoyant, not overwhelmed. Stress levels maintained at a point where they are not overflowing.

'A routine for the mind, rather than the body,' she says.

They have to be things you are naturally drawn to because you enjoy them, rather than things that feel like a chore. An absolutely bespoke plan, created by you, for you.

She's talking about self-care essentially. But this is self-care beyond the candle-lit bubble bath of social media. Maria is nothing if not practical, and so is her plan. *She is granular*, I think, using the word currently in favour in the media to describe an interview heavy on detail. But, in Maria's case, I mean she is literally of the earth, a grounding type of person.

'In a crisis, you do whatever you need to,' she tells me. 'But if you have a wellness plan already in place, then it really clicks in when you are under duress.'

The world of wellness comes in for a lot of bashing. What I am talking about is not something that involves spending large amounts of money on dubious products (although go for it, if that's your thing) or alternative medical practices. It is simply habits, practices and rituals that make you feel well in your mind.

And more than that, it seems to me a world in which women come together to support one another.

Apart from a brief skirmish with glory as the centre-forward in our First Year hockey team, I have never been sporty. It was a short-lived moment – my apparent prowess was actually due to tips given by an older, genuinely sporty cousin before school began. Everyone else quickly caught up with how to dribble a ball. And, ever since, I have not considered myself the sporty kind.

But then I had probably (definitely) also thought years later that I was not the divorcing kind either ...

And then, in the months preceding our wedding, I went to a trainer three times a week, sometimes getting up as early as five o'clock. Eventually, I hung from a bar and managed to pull myself up in mid-air. Things I would never have thought possible from myself.

For a time, I became the kind of person who occasionally ate dinner leftovers for breakfast (I still swear by a boiled egg in chilli con carne any time of the day). I even drank a few protein shakes (revolting). And I have never in my life felt so free of worry, anxiety or headaches as I did in those few months.

Since our daughter was born, I had been attempting to get back to training with little success.

Our daughter was a dreadful sleeper, still often waking on the hour, every hour almost six months in. I mentioned the attempts to return to the trainer to my mother, appointments at six in the morning, heading into rush-hour traffic to get home before work, and was met with yet another withering glance and barely concealed eye roll. 'I don't know why you're bothering with this right now,' she muttered.

I finally admitted defeat one morning after we had

been awake for four hours in the middle of the night, ahead of a 7 a.m. appointment to train. I waited until five in the morning, for maximum dramatic effect.

'She is still awake, we have been for hours, I won't make it.'

And that was the end of exercise for some time.

Now, after the initial months after of my marriage breakdown, I need everything I can get – and I know exercise will make me feel better. So, as a kickstart to my own wellness plan, I rejoin my local gym and tell myself to just go. Not every day or a set number of days; just some days.

When I am there, I can do whatever I want. No pressure. Run for ten minutes. Hell, don't even run; walk. Lift weights on one machine and then leave. Some days, I just sit in the kids' ball-pit area with my daughter and Sophie and her boys. Sophie and I chat, the kids roll about, and I tell myself that I have been in the environment of exercise. A sort of contact high. And that, for now, is enough.

When you go through a crisis, there is little, if anything, left over for the extras of life. That I am slowly able to even imagine such a thing is possible, something that will require effort being applied to things other than my child or work, is the first sign that we are moving away from ground zero.

Chapter 26

Macro and Micro

I decided that my wellness plan would have both a macro and a micro level. The micro level is stuff I told myself I would do on a weekly basis, things I knew I would enjoy. Coffee with a friend. A walk. The gym. Eating as well as I could. Sophie and I began to work in the lobby of our gym, so that we could, through power of mutual peer pressure, try and get each other upstairs to spend twenty minutes on the treadmill.

But I am determined that none of this will become a stick with which to beat myself, if I don't do it, so be it. This is not a to-do list. Rather a collection of suggestions ready for me to turn to should the mood, and the energy levels, take me.

And then there will be the macro stuff. It doesn't

matter how amicable your separation is, nobody gets through it without experiencing huge levels of stress. But like the frog slowly boiling in the water, when you are in the middle of it, you don't necessarily realise just how stressed you are.

I was stressed. Terminally stressed, it felt at one point. And I needed to release some of the pressure. I needed big jolts out of everyday life that would bring down my stress levels because when you are this wired, you cannot take them down yourself.

I made a deal with myself, that I will not let more than three months go by without one of these pressure releases. It might be going away, or it might be simply a night out with friends, and the entire next day in bed myself, with nothing to do but read and snooze. Even the knowing that it is coming – that a break is booked in – helps to get through the times in between.

Chapter 27

Mantra, Mantra, Mantra ... What Am I Having for Breakfast?

For years, my mother had been badgering me to take up meditation and, for years, I had been ignoring her, as is the way with things your mother urges you to do. Until, that is, I found myself with a marriage that had fallen apart and stress levels that were off the charts, and I knew I needed to do something.

I came across a newspaper article about the London Meditation Centre (LMC). A deep dive into the journalist's Instagram account revealed a beautiful country-abode-yoga-in-the-kitchen-filled life. There's a picture with the article, a white, wisteria-clad mews in Kensington where the meditation course she attended is held. Sash windows. A cobbled street. It looks like something out of a Richard Curtis movie. *This is it*, I thought. *This is the one*. Nothing too incense-filled, nothing too hempy. This is where I will learn how to meditate.

The day I booked the course was the first of September, a crisply cold day, with the type of golden sun that comes at you from a slant rather than on high. It happened to be our wedding anniversary and also the day we finally decided, definitively, that there was no going back for us.

On the radio, Fintan O'Toole is talking about Brexit. 'They're nostalgic for a future Britain will never have,' he says. 'They and me both,' I think, contemplating the future I will not now have. Although right then, I would have given anything for an emotion as gentle as nostalgia.

I am sitting in my car outside my house, trying to work myself up to call the LMC. Wondering if this horrible confluence of fate would ever not feel almost unbearably grim. These two events happening on this one day. Later, I found a friend who had been through the same thing; the decision to separate made on their fifth wedding anniversary. We marvelled at the coincidence, then realised that actually it made sense in a way because, if your marriage is trouble, then the thought of faking your way through a big anniversary can be the straw that breaks things.

Looking back two years later, I could have told myself that the next year would still feel horribly grim, but easier, a sort of grit-your-teeth-and-get-through-it day, but that the year after that would feel surprisingly OK.

That things that felt like they would always hurt terribly, wouldn't anymore.

On that day, though, it just felt awful.

'You're so stressed,' my mother would say again and again at that time.

'I'm not, I'm fine,' I would reply. What I really meant was *I'm coping. I'm still going. I'm not falling apart.*

What I couldn't even quite articulate was that admitting how stressed I was felt impossible. Useless really. What would be the point when it felt like there was nothing that could be done? Nowhere for that knowledge to go if I put it out there, except for it to solidify as yet another layer on top of everything else I was carrying. Where would that stress go? Admitting to the amount of stress I felt would simply make it more tangible, more of a burden; it certainly wouldn't lessen it.

So I buried it. I pushed through.

Sometimes when you are deep within a difficult time, there is nothing you can do to calm yourself or replenish yourself. You need others to do it for you. To take down the stress, or hold it for you momentarily. Doing it for yourself is not possible. This is when I realise that I need to insert the first big pressure valve of my wellness plan. The something big which would help me to stop from imploding.

I get through to Michael, who, with his wife – the beautifully named Jill Lavender – runs the LMC.

'What do you want to get out of this?' Michael asks quietly.

Almost immediately, I start crying down the phone, sitting in the car outside the house. 'I'm so sorry,' I sob, struggling to get the words out. 'Today is our wedding anniversary. It's a difficult day.'

Michael is utterly nonplussed by this outpouring. I like him immediately.

My daughter, my parents and I go to London for a long weekend. I will go to the course each morning, and we will visit my friend Shereen and do touristy things every afternoon. A Paddington movie has just been released and we are staying beside the Tower of London; my daughter can't quite believe it when she spots it from our taxi. We are staying at my cousin's apartment, all white, oatmeal and pale blue interiors, exposed brick and metal pipes, and I immediately start fantasy-redecorating our home, ignoring the fact that I barely have the energy to put out the bins.

Leaving the apartment early on the first day – even setting off on my own in a new city – feels uplifting, a reprieve from the sadness. A small chance to pretend for the length of a Tube ride that I am living a different life.

When I arrive at the LMC, I hand over the bunch of flowers we had been asked to bring. My mother had bought my flowers that morning in the local shop while I gave my daughter breakfast – I had barely glanced at them apart from to vaguely take in that they were small yellow roses.

Having divested ourselves of shoes and coats, we enter the main room, and are told to locate our flowers, which have each been laid at a chair, and to sit down.

Jesus. I have no idea which are mine, I think. I contemplate having to admit to the class that my mother bought mine. How un-meditation. How barely even bloody adult. As it turns out, half the group has also bought theirs in Tesco Express, so we all make our way cautiously to a chair with a bunch of small yellowy-orange roses.

Things start with a short ceremony. The group is gathered together at one side of the room, each of us clutching a bunch of flowers, while our two teachers stand together before an altar, chanting in what I guess is Sanskrit.

I panic immediately. *Will there be audience participation? How did I so entirely forget the kind of person I am?* I wail inwardly to myself. Which is to say, the kind of person who detests any sort of overt ceremony, who has an overly developed cringe response. Who finds any kind of showy displays of spirituality suspect.

I start to wonder if a discreet exit is possible. We're on the door side of the room. *I could probably make it*, I think.

Only the thought of my mother, to whom I have just

said goodbye on the other side of that door, keeps me rooted where I am.

Thankfully, the ceremony is soon over and we return to our seats, where Michael reveals himself to be a thoroughly sensible sort of person; witty, a little sarcastic. Our course is in Vedic meditation, which, he explains, is a form developed in India thousands of years ago. It was created for what they called 'householders' – multitasking working people, rather than those living a monastic, spiritual life. As a non-spiritual-atheist-soon-to-be-single-mother-self-employed-person, this feels spot on.

After the introductory chat, it is time for each of us to be given our mantra. One by one, Jill leads us to another room where Michael now sits. When my turn comes, we stand together in a quiet corridor, she an ombre vision in various shades of muted grey, like something out of *The Lord of the Rings*.

'Sometimes, meditation comes to people when they need it most,' she murmurs softly, looking off into the distance.

'Sometimes, it takes a little bit of a crisis for people to step out of their usual mode of functioning because that usual mode isn't working anymore,' Michael explains further when I ask him about it later. 'It's no longer serving them. And they might be open to doing something outside their personal norm. When someone gets cracked open, they're open.'

It's surprisingly soothing; the feeling of having placed myself in the hands of someone who knows what they're doing. Of my wellbeing not being my responsibility for this short time. Not my job to maintain.

On day two, we sit and meditate. Afterwards Michael goes around the class asking each of us how much time they think has passed. Guesses range between two and five minutes. It had been twenty.

Michael talks about meditation erasing past hurts. The bigger the hurt buried within you, the more meditations are needed to exercise it. A cumulative effect. *How many meditations does it take to erase the hurt of a marriage break up?* I wonder.

I had tried the apps and tried just plonking down in a corner of my room and thinking of nothing for ten minutes. Neither had worked. Something about Michael's approach, the conviction with which he spoke about the effects of meditation, paired with the simplicity of it, an attitude of unpreciousness, that it's no big deal, meant that this time, it worked.

'Mantra, mantra, mantra, mantra – What am I having for breakfast? – mantra, mantra,' he says, describing an anecdote Jerry Seinfeld tells about how he meditates. Your mind wanders but it is no big deal. You simply go back to the mantra. Some members of the class try to dissect the process, or their own performance of it, and I can see Michael gently trying to show them, 'It doesn't matter. Don't overthink it, just do it.'

I've grown up watching my mother meditate. Barging into her room every so often to find her sitting quietly on her bed, something I now, as a fully-fledged meditator, realise must have been deeply jarring. It turns out that this means that, to me, it is no big deal, I take to it with unexpected ease.

'What's your mantra?" my mother immediately asks gleefully when she meets me after class, a look of a naughty child on her face. Many years ago, she had attended a course in Kerry with a group of friends. On the bus home afterwards, some of the group revealed mantras, only to discover half of them had been given the same one. RAM. 'I can't possibly tell you that,' I bluster pompously. 'Meditating rule 101.'

'I loved it,' I admit, and I can see that she is making a conscious effort to keep the smug I-told-you-so look from her face, and to not immediately urge me to read *The Power of Now*, her other favourite. She comes to class with me the next day, at the invitation of Michael – during the first day, he had asked each person how they first came across the practice and was delighted when I related that my mother had been meditating for years. He announces her to the group as a meditator of over forty years and a ripple of awe passes through the room, at which she looks serenely pleased with herself, a person who is taking this as simply her due.

'Each of you is like an onion,' Michael tells us. To begin, we are peeling off the layers of stress. I spend the week of the course with a splitting headache, but it feels like the stress of months is exiting my body in waves. 'The onion is the layers of stress,' Michael explains. 'First there's deep fatigue, like when you go on holiday and collapse for the first eighteen hours because you didn't realise how tired you actually were until you slowed down a bit. We're covering up the fatigue, and when we slow down, it shows up.'

One day in, I already sense the difference. It is as if I have been encased within a full-body coating of insulation, wrapped in my own invisible lagging jacket. Things are still difficult, but there is an epidermis layer right at the surface which cannot be touched by it all. Things can bother me, but only so much. Deep within, I am cocooned.

All week, I crave green juice, spend ridiculous amounts on the stuff. As if some need within me for nourishment has been unearthed beneath the layers of tension.

'Stress has a masking effect on the senses,' Michael tells me. 'And then, when we take that away, we start to detect what it is we actually want or what the body actually needs. Meditation bankrupts your ability to ignore.'

Try and relax in the afternoon, Michael tells us. *Unlikely*, I think. We go to the Natural History Museum, stand in awe under the whale, my daughter and mother go on the merry-go-round outside, screaming in excitement. We visit Shereen and her family, and her husband entertains the girls while Shereen and my mother and I do a turbo catch-up on the couch.

It's the first time I have seen my friend since the split. It feels like there is a before and an after now, and I have got myself into the after. It's not particularly pleasant, but it's an achievement of sorts, if an exhausting one right now.

We are instructed to meditate twice a day, ideally first thing in the morning and then some time after lunch, so our entire day happens through the calming filter of the practice.

The first time I cannot do this is the day we fly home, and the morning feels like nails being slowly dragged down a blackboard. Admittedly, I am flying with a small child, an event in itself capable of producing such a feeling. But it is more than that. I feel raw. As if my nerve ends are exposed for all to rub against. Michael says this is how stressed we feel pretty much all of the time, we only notice it when we put the barrier of meditation between ourselves and our stress. We are used to it. *Sounds about right*, I think.

Chapter 28

The Child Inside

If you had told me two years earlier that I would be talking about my inner child with a real sense of conviction, I would have presumed that this whole divorce thing had broken me, that I had taken leave of my senses. And yet, here I was.

When the fear about the future, or about my ability to keep us afloat, or my daughter's wellbeing, became overwhelming, going to Judith was the thing that helped the most.

Judith is an author, a theologian, a kinesiologist, and a life coach. Sophie first met her when she was sent to interview her; I muscle in on the territory shortly afterwards. In person, Judith is a beauty who looks like a folk singer from the 1960s. The fact that she is also separated and a mother is hugely helpful. She speaks from direct experience. 'I remember looking in the mirror and thinking, *Well that's me done. Where do I go from here?* I was forty-one at the time,' she tells me of when her own marriage ended, almost a decade ago. Needless to say, she was far from done.

A session involves talking mostly. What is going on, how will we deal with it. On one occasion, I arrive slightly bent over from pains in my stomach that had been going on since the night before. At first, I put them down to having scoffed the remains of my daughter's party bag brought home from a birthday party, instead of dinner.

Meant to be meeting friends, I had driven halfway there and had to return as the pains worsened.

'Food poisoning?' I suggested to my mother and she looked dubious, because she knows that it is not. Things were stressful at the time, I was especially worried about an event the next day after my meeting with Judith. I walked into her rooms slightly hunched over and burst into tears at the sight of her.

She put me up on the bed in her inner office, wrapped me in blankets, and told me to close my eyes as she stood over me. I'm not really sure what she did next, but the pains vanished.

I ask her if fear is a big issue for the people she sees. She lowers her chin slightly to emphasise the directness of the look she is giving me, and says, 'Fear is everything. Fear is what blocks us. We can use other words – depression, anxiety, anger – but I use the blanket word of fear. Everything is fear.'

She describes her own fear, in the aftermath of her own marriage breakdown. 'To deal with your fear,' she says, 'you need to talk to your inner child. I had to go back and find my inner child, and love her to pieces. I had made myself outward facing, looking at everybody else, pleasing everybody else. I had to turn inwards.'

It sounds mad, inner child, but, actually, when you look at it, all it means is that there is the fearful child you, and there is the adult, able-for-it you. And the one talks the other down.

'Talk to your inner child,' Judith tells me. 'You're OK – we'll step through this.'

You soothe your fear like you would a child, because like a child, your subconscious reacts to the feeling of comforting and minding and soothing, Judith tells me. 'You can be surrounded by loads and loads of people and still be really scared. You have to be able to do it for yourself. You have to go back in and tell that little girl inside you, 'I have you, I'm minding you.' Mind her and love her and protect her.'

I spend the next week walking around with my hand patting my chest where I think my heart is, just as Judith has taught me, I catch myself doing it walking up Grafton Street one day on my way to an interview; marching along, right hand patting my heart, muttering to myself, 'You are OK, nothing can harm you, everything will pass.' I think how mad this must look, and then how I don't care because it is making me feel better. And the thing is, it might (probably does) look odd, but it takes the fear down. It settles me from being all jangle-ragged nerve endings and a mind that races about after itself.

My cousin-the-psychologist, to whom I refer for a second opinion on all things, tells me we all have our vulnerable child inside us. And we also have our adult self. The thing is to know that the vulnerable child will always be there, she explains – in the form of fear, anger, anxiety, whatever your personal bugbear – and for the adult self to know how to comfort and reassure it, rather than fight it, or expect it to go away forever. To be afraid, but enable yourself to do the things anyway.

'What about the times when I feel like I cannot do it for myself?' I ask Judith. And she tells me that I am only beginning to restore a reserve now, and that I will not always feel so easily overwhelmed. 'The more you do these things,' she says, 'the meditation, the walking, the whatever-it-is-that-works-for-you, the more of a reserve you build up.'

And I believe her, because she has been exactly where I am now, but no longer is.

I tell her how sometimes at the park, the sight of families together gives me an overwhelming sense of sadness. And she smiles because, after nine years, she had so totally forgotten feeling like that. 'Only for you saying that, I would never have remembered I ever felt like that. Everything evolves in a different way and nothing really stays the same anyway,' she says.

'You're at that point, and I know that point, where your head is just coming out of the well,' Judith says. 'You were down at the bottom of the well, and you had to pull yourself out. You thought, *There's daylight up there somewhere, but I don't even know where it is*, and then you clawed your way up, holding your child on your back. You slid down again, and then you crawled back up. You will get over the top of the well and then you're back in your life. And it's your life, and it's the way you want it. It's a completion. You will feel satisfied in you.'

Chapter 29

Food, Glorious Food

Very early on, my daughter and I instigated a tradition of Friday-night takeaway – chicken tikka masala, or chicken mikka masala, as my daughter calls it.

A tradition is also a way of saying that, by Friday afternoon, I am exhausted and cannot face the prospect of cooking yet another dinner. My admittedly meagre list of meals that my daughter will eat and which you get two days out of deserts me after Thursday. We go to Bombay Pantry, where they know our order, the two of us single-minded in our favourite, never diverting. It's both embarrassing and touching. 'Grandad not with you today?' they will ask, if it is just the two of us. They see us coming now and reach for the brown paper bag of poppadoms they give my daughter as a gift.

Our weekly takeaway is a pat on the back to us both, for getting to Friday. It gets me off the hook for an evening from the relentless dinner, bath, bedtime round. I realise now, much later, that setting up a tradition is a sign of confidence in the new life. A friend tells me that, in the aftermath of her family falling apart, she was scared to set up new traditions for years afterwards, for fear of making something that would somehow break up again.

At first, it can occasionally feel bleak, just the two of us on a Friday night. A unit missing an essential part. If I'm particularly tired, my brain likes to torture itself with visions of my cousin's house nearby, imagining her family's garrulous domestic bliss.

I worry I am letting my daughter down, making a takeaway part of our definite routine. As if fish fingers, McDonalds or pizza wouldn't have passed her lips if we hadn't separated. 'It's all good stuff isn't it?' I enquire of the staff for the thousandth time. 'Basically cream and tomatoes?'

But soon I grow to love it. How my daughter looks forward all week to curry night. Our shared passion for this meal, which we would both eat every night if allowed. The sense of a small hurdle having been crossed for having got through the week. We pop to the shop next door while we wait for our order and discuss what we will have for breakfast the next morning, bicker gently over whether or not she can get a magazine, pick out the berries to go with the next day's pancakes if we're going to Sophie's for breakfast.

In the aftermath of the split, our dinner table becomes ground zero in the mission to put things back together. The foundation of our building site. Even when things are at their worst, you still have to cook and eat, so food seems like as good a place as any to start. Bricks and mortar.

'I don't like change', says just about everyone. Is it really, though, that we don't like a lack of control? We'll change if we want to, but when it is foisted upon us, we resist? Who wants that? A change we would not have chosen, if we could be in charge of exactly how our lives would go.

So, in the midst of a big, sad, scary change, that even though you knew it was the right thing you would never have wished for yourself, you grab at the small things, eke out little corners within your life, where you can exert a modicum of control.

As my due date approached, my husband and I had earnestly made a catalogue of weekly meals and a shopping list of all the ingredients they would require; a futile effort to even slightly thwart the oncoming onslaught of a newborn, and the havoc we knew was about to be wreaked upon our lives. As if a freezer packed full of homemade meals would mean sailing through the newborn stage.

I interview a woman who tells me that she became a

vegetarian after the death of her father. Now, after the death of her husband, her daughter has become vegan. Both of them trying to exert a modicum of control in the face of the greatest disregarder of human attempts to achieve an upper hand. When confronted by loss, you grab on to anything you can control. It's a way of feeling comforted; that there are still some things over which you have agency.

On the first night my husband is in his new home, it seems important to have dinner at the table, rather than to eat it collapsed in exhaustion watching TV. It is a Wednesday, roast chicken with Grandad night, an evening when my husband would have been working late anyway.

I make the meal, serve it, and watch my daughter and father chat; there are great deliberations over the addition of pepper and salt. I am mostly silent, contributing little to the conversation. I have made the meal, that will have to do as my part. My father covers for me, calm as always. And even in the midst of all that is happening, it is satisfying, to have achieved this little bit of keeping-things-going. *I put dinner on the table, a dinner that will give us leftovers for tomorrow no less*, I think smugly.

Food is a way back to a sense of control. A way of proving that we are still a family.

Our dinner table becomes command centre, the war room from which I will rebuild. I don't subscribe to the idea that it is essential to sit down every night as a family at the dinner table, so that table is a moveable feast; sometimes at the actual dining-room table, sometimes the kitchen island, sometimes the couch and, on Saturdays, it moves to my bed for movie night.

My own family gave up on dinners at the dinner table somewhere in my early teens, instead we all sat down together to watch *The Simpsons*, dinner plates on our knees.

We're fine.

So I'm not getting caught up in guilt that if my daughter and I do not sit at the actual table each night, development is doomed. When you fall outside the nuclear way of things, then the upside is you get to make things up for yourself. We are living off grid now. We do what works for us.

'We're *never* allowed food upstairs in our house,' one of my daughter's playdates tells me in that stern, judgmental tone small children adopt when they have caught you out. 'Off you go,' I reply briskly, resisting the urge to argue my case with a four-year-old and shoving the ice-cream treats into their hands. 'We do things differently around here.' The food on this occasion buys me a ten-minute window to answer work emails.

Your new normal needn't look anything like what is generally considered 'normal'. You do whatever works best for you. You are unconstrained by norms.

And so, our dinner table is mutable. On the occasional Saturday morning at the start of school holidays, it is her bed. My daughter lies with her eyes closed, pretending to be asleep, but beaming, while I arrive with her food, I can hear her giggling as I come up the stairs. 'Don't come in, don't come in,' she shouts, and there is frantic rustling of blankets while she hides.

Food becomes a framework around which I create our new life. Both a pillar that supports it and then, a little later, a beam upon whose weight I test our ability to be a twosome, both in company and alone.

I use food to test and then confirm that we are OK as we move through the months afterwards.

Are we strong enough yet to contemplate hosting? Or to sit down, just the two of us, for a lazy weekend breakfast and not feel that something is lacking?

With Saturday pancakes, we learn how to have a slow morning together, not forced to rush out the door unthinkingly on the school run. And for this to be a nice thing; the morning unfolding unplanned before us, the weekend still fully ahead, a thing to be relished.

Am I strong enough to host a dinner party on my own? To send my daughter to her grandparents for a slumber party and have friends over? To watch those friends leave at the end of the night and for it to be just me – and to not feel sad?

I try it out with my schoolfriends, an easy meal of things to be picked at. Beforehand, I pace nervously, changing the lighting arrangements, the background music, like a person preparing for a first date rather than the arrival of women she's known all her life. They arrive in a gang, and it is as if nothing has changed, with these women, most of whom I have known since we were four. When they leave, I think only of the morning and how I will relish not being awake from seven.

Meals become miniature celebrations of our new life. Breakfasts at Sophie's, the children playing around us, fuelled by pancakes, berries and endless snacks. Sunday lunches at my parents. Seafront walks with my brother, ending in dinner at our favourite restaurant, and an ice-cream almost the size of her head, raspberry ripple running down over her hands. 'I love it,' she drawls. 'Best night ever.'

A few weeks after the split, when I have not managed a food shop, breakfast becomes pancakes in a restaurant before playschool. It feels like a very single-mum fail, to have nothing to feed her for breakfast, but I decide to style it out, announcing grandly that we're going out.

Coffees, a big-girl 'cino – *not* a babycino my daughter will say indignantly if she hears me whispering it to the waiter – and thick banana cake at Olive's room stables in the park, my daughter playing in the courtyard with her friends, while Lewine and I drink our coffees.

Some Sunday mornings, when I am too tired to play, but feel guilty about turning on the TV, we take ourselves to our local Starbucks, which, along with

Lidl, is the most exciting thing to happen in years to our neighbourhood. The staff are sweet to her, they miss my frantic waving not to and pile her 'cino high with marshmallows. And she plays and we chat and I read the newspaper.

If a week has been particularly challenging, I take comfort from feeding my daughter homemade food. Don't get me wrong. This isn't an ode to an organic-only, all-food-made-from-scratch, lifestyle. I have no compunction in turning to pizzas and fish fingers. In the summer months, when we're out and about all the time, we live on them, eking out extra hours for an outing, rather than heading home early to start preparing dinner. But if I feel like I am struggling on multiple fronts, or in the weeks when it feels particularly hard that the life I wanted has gotten so far away from us, watching my daughter eat something I made gives me comfort.

My banana muffins made of porridge and honey become a lunchbox staple and, to me only, a sign that I am coping.

I can make them in five minutes, before the school run if I need, while I get us both ready to leave, a triumph in its own right – the single mother who bakes before the school run, take *that* nuclear family. It's a blow when she eventually looks at her lunchbox one day, and says, in the manner of one explaining things to a simpleton, that she cannot eat them any longer. 'I've eaten them all my life, Mommy.'

One morning, I realise halfway through that we have no bananas. I substitute raspberries and the result is a soupy mess, so I pick up a pastry at the Insomnia next door to her school, explaining to her teacher as I hand over the lunches. 'I don't know why you bother,' she says kindly to my story of morning baking.

'Because it makes me feel like I am doing right by my daughter,' I do not say out loud.

Chapter 30

Scenes from the Hole

I start to leave Sophie a voice note, something meaningless that I've just spotted on Instagram, but suddenly my voice goes hoarse and I'm crying. Everything feels too much. And like it will always feel too much. The juggle, the balancing, the co-parenting, the financial worry, the fear over the future. I delete the note. Crawl back into my cave of avoiding everyone.

*

I know I should ring Helen the counsellor but I don't. Crying it all out right now seems to require energy I don't have. It feels easier to keep going.

*

We are at the musical *Annie*. On stage, the actress sings 'Tomorrow', and my daughter, in a red dress with a crisp white collar, sings along. And the plaintive song, and the childish innocence, kills me. I start crying, cannot stop. My mother distracts her.

*

Right now, as I write this. My life feels too much, like an unbearable pressure weighing down on me. I wake at night and am instantly alert, the anxiety feels like a rod of kryptonite taking up all my insides, crammed in there giving me indigestion, so big it feels impossible to breathe properly.

*

Signs you are in the hole:

1. Finding you are crying, and that you hadn't really noticed you had started.
2. Avoiding friends.
3. Feeling you do not have the time or energy to do the things you know have helped in the past.
4. Not being able to ring your best friends, because you know that at the sounds of their voices you will start crying.
5. Ditto your mother.
6. An inability to know you are in the hole.
7. Doing the avoidance dance; 'I'm just busy/tired/hungover.'

8. Reading articles with titles like 'Five Signs You're Nearing Breaking Point' and almost relishing the fact that you can match each symptom. But not doing anything about it.

*

Sidenote: there can be a small plus side to being in the hole. Somewhere, a tiny part of you might realise that you're approaching dgaf (Don't Give a Fu*k) territory. There can be a type of bravery to be found in that. Grab this part, and use it as a launch pad to push you past your fears.

*

It is OK to let things fall apart. It will be OK. You will be OK. People will catch you. Someone will reach out and catch you. Some will even get down into the hole with you and help to dig you out. The friend who knows just by the tone of your voice that you are not OK, and who will come and check in on you. One of them, your mother maybe, will even lift you out when you cannot do it for yourself.

Chapter 31

The Slumber Party

It is the morning of the first day on which my daughter will spend the night at her father's, something she is going to do weekly. She wakes and stretches like a kitten, yawning, before reaching over to paw my cheek with the flat of her hand in the dark. I almost text her father there and then to say she's sick, she has to stay home.

'This is a good thing,' I tell myself. 'A break for me – a good thing. Time with her dad – a good thing.'

In theory.

In reality, part of me wants to keep her from playschool and spend the day on the couch under the duvet watching movies.

I pull myself together.

'This is a good thing,' I tell myself again.

And really, I know it is. Maybe earlier, I would have taken this as a terrible sign of how badly things had gone wrong. How wildly off course we were; my baby, sleeping under another roof once a week. But now, this feels like PMS. Hormonal upset you know will definitely pass.

We get ready to leave, and I can't stop touching her. Pulling her jumper down just so at the waist, and then running my hands down her sides, her back and belly. Patting her. Tucking her in as if she is a bed I am making.

I end up feeding her her cereal like she is a baby. 'Open up for the train,' I squeal with hysterical undertones, and she gives me a witheringly pitying sideways look that, if she knew the phrase, would say, *Mommy, get a grip*.

Actually, it's quite possible she does know the phrase – only the day before she informed me at dinner that frankly, she disagreed with what I was saying.

I pull myself together.

I catch a glimpse of her side profile, her head is angled slightly downward, and the sight of her babyish chubby double chin almost breaks me.

In a fit of denial that this is happening, I am trying to avoid any appearance of luggage, so I compress her things into a tiny bag within her playschool bag, but the box of her favourite cereal we have bought for her to bring won't fit and so another is required. What with the new cushion we are bringing for circle time, we're now in full-on luggage mode.

'This is not a big deal. You need the break. This is a good thing,' I tell myself.

As I trudge resentfully into playschool in the wake of her scooter, I hear them before I see them, the father saying, 'Now that's another way of using the phrase 'excuse me',' and, in my foul mood, I think, *Ugh, other parents and their earnestness; the absolute worst.*

Then they catch up with us, and mine stops. 'Hi, I'm Sarah,' she announces to the other child, as usual a one-woman social committee. 'You're in my gym class.'

The father's face breaks open in a smile of relief and gratitude. His little girl is new to the playschool; this is her first day. And I can see how much it means to him, my daughter claiming his as a friend. And I see that I'm not the only person hovering over their child in a state of anxiety. The two girls chat below us, oblivious to the clouds of parental angst floating above their heads.

'After school sports?' her teacher asks innocently as I hand the extra bag over.

I barely make it back out the door, have to barrel my way through other parents. I reach the safety of the car where Adele, of course, comes on the radio. *OK, so,* I think. *Let's do this*, and bawl to 'When We Were Young' all the way home.

This is a good thing. You get a lie in in the morning. You need a break.

I make myself remember my friend Lucy, also separated, who told me that she wishes someone had told her at the start to use this time. *Rest. Look after yourself.* I allow my memory of this to tell me to do just that.

I bump into another mum at the shop. 'Awwww-nnnnn,' she says when I blurt out her at her what is going on. I instantly regret saying anything. 'You poor thing,' she continues, head-tilting until her ear nearly touches her shoulder.

'Not to worry,' I snap. 'Sure, she's home with me all afternoon every other day. Where's yours? Oh in crèche?' And I march off defiantly. It's a low blow, I feel instantly guilty. I don't approve of this kind of thing, competitive mothering. And I don't care what arrangement anyone else has; everyone does what works best for them and their family. But she got me at a bad moment.

I get home and spend much of the afternoon sitting on the couch, working and WhatsApping my mums-group, friends since our children were six weeks old. It's a sort of private live-tweeting of my day.

It's such a treat not to have to think about what I'll do for dinner. I'm off the dinner-bath-bedtime carousel. Might just make toast.

15.19

Actually, I'm going out with Sophie for dinner.
15.30

Might have a nap first.
16.01

Just had a twenty-minute shower, considering painting my nails.
17.07

It's not all easy. Sometimes it's not easy at all. Dropping your small child to their classroom door and saying 'see you tomorrow' never fails to feel jarring. Sometimes, a day will have gone swimmingly and then, at six o'clock, I will be hit by how much I miss her, feel suddenly undone and at a loss, and have to go lie on her bed. I swing between being delighted to be off the routine and not knowing what to do with myself.

And I think that it is easier for me because it is just one night. I tell myself it's the equivalent of going out straight after work, if I was in an office, and leaving early for a meeting the next day. And I know that she has a ball at her father's, wakes up on the morning and often first thing exclaims with delight, 'Daddy-daughter day.'

I learn to have things at the ready for those times when the missing her feels too much. A book, a movie, a friend ready to go. Routines already established to fall back on.

But as time goes on, my preference is to spend the

evening at home on my own. It's nice to have some time entirely to myself. Sometimes, it feels like future proofing against a time when I will live on my own – though this is unnecessary future thinking, I know Helen the counsellor would tell me.

But it's mainly because sometimes when I go out, coming home to an empty house feels too lonely, and I miss her too much, for all that I enjoy putting on the TV full volume, and walking without watching my step up our wooden stairs, because she is not there to wake.

My current favourite own-time routine is beef in black-bean sauce from our local Thai takeaway while listening to a podcast and watching an Agatha Christie drama in the background. Sometimes, I work until twelve, and get up the next morning at six to work again. It makes the rest of the week seem more balanced, means I can take the next afternoon off to spend with her.

Swings and roundabouts.

That first night, though, I go and meet Sophie for dinner. She has guessed that I would need something to do.

'How was it?' she asks on my arrival.

'It was terrific,' I reply. 'I had a nap.'

Chapter 32

The Question of Failure

I know it is common, almost expected, to feel soul-crushing levels of failure when a marriage breaks down. And I get that, of course. I just didn't feel it. When you have tried very hard to make something work and it does not work, and you both subsequently face that rather terrifying reality that it is over, I think it feels like the opposite of being a failure.

But maybe that is just delusion on a grand scale, and a tsunami of feelings of failure await me in the wings.

It is easy when your relationship ends or when you become a single parent to feel othered. Your life has failed. You go off in your corner and feel different from the rest of your world. Grief alone will do that to you. You feel raw; both a downer to the world around you, but also resentful of their OK-ness.

At first, you need others who are in exactly the same situation as you to make you feel better, but I think also, if you are lucky, you need and get others who are in, seemingly at least, totally different situations.

Sometimes, at the start, the rightness of their life might highlight the wrongness of yours when you are still in deep denial. That can be helpful, in alerting you to the fact that something needs to change.

Later, you will see that even though they have what you are missing, they might be struggling with other things.

When my daughter was a few weeks old, my mother forced me to go to a mum and baby's breastfeeding group. I complained the entire way there in the car.

'I don't need new friends,' I whined like a petulant child.

'I have friends with kids,' I objected.

'I'm not a joiner,' I said crossly.

Still friends almost forty years later with the women from her own group, she blithely ignored me. Because she knew the importance of women who are in the trenches with you at the exact same moment, whether that be grief, new single parenthood or becoming a mother.

Maybe this is the voice of a separated woman speaking, but I think that in those early baby days, you need your female friends as much, more even, than your fellow parent.

You share the hard labour with your partner, the physical work of the thing, passing the baby between you. But emotional support? You're no good to each other. You're like expert rugby players, you and your fellow parent, passing the child back and forth to each other while also jealously clocking who has had most reading-their-phone-in-the-bathroom time.

'We came up for breath seven months in, went for a dinner and realised we'd barely looked each other in the eye since she was born,' a friend says after her second was born. When you become a mother, and you feel like you are failing, only another mother can look at you and say, 'I know, I felt the same'. When your marriage falls apart, it is only another woman who can look you in the eye and say, 'I know, me too', and take away that feeling that you are utterly alone and uniquely lacking.

I chose a different hill to die on when it comes to failure. My daughter had reflux as a baby, the only thing that would stop her crying and put her to sleep was rocking.

'Did you rock her to sleep in your arms?' a visiting acquaintance asked judgily a few weeks later.

You try it, I want to say. Seven. Hours. Of. Screaming. And then the screaming after every feed. You'd do *anything* to stop it.

Looking back now, I realise that it was just one of those things that happen – my daughter arrived with reflux – but, at the time, it felt infused with personal failure.

So I had always felt slightly like a failure in front of my breastfeeding mums. Or, at least, I spent most of the first year of our friendship feeling like a failure. And then I grew out of it, as I became more confident as a mother. And now, even though none of them are separated and they are all on their subsequent babies since the ones that brought us together, I do not feel alienated from them.

They are my ultimate compare-and-contrast litmus testers.

On nights out before the split, one of them would mention in passing some domestic detail between herself and her husband, and it would jar with me, for being so different from how things were in my own home. It helped me to realise that things were not right. Something that would have been easily ignored if I were more isolated.

I know that comparison is the death of happiness. But. If you get up close to people, you see that most of us are carrying something, and comparison can be comforting.

Now, after the split, I know that although they are within the 2.4 bubble and I am without, there is other stuff that brings us together. They have stuff to deal with. We all do. Their stuff might not look exactly like mine – and you do need people whose stuff *is* exactly the same as yours –but they have stuff to deal with too. Loss. Stress. Frustration.

Grief and motherhood. Both will break open your world. You need people who get that.

On a more prosaic level, when there isn't another parent in the house, you need to get your barometer of what is normal – your reassurance – from elsewhere.

'Do you guys ever scream back when your kid loses it and screams at you?' I ask tentatively one morning, as we sit around coffees, the children in school. I am trying to sound casual and matter of fact, afraid they might be horrified.

For a moment, they all look shocked.

But the shock is not at the situation I'm describing, but that I would have to ask. It's a hard yes from around the table.

Chapter 33

Boundaries

Now I can't quite believe this, but there was a time when I genuinely didn't understand what people meant when they talked about 'boundaries'. Of course, I understood a physical boundary – one you could see. I could point you out a fence or a wall.

But emotional boundaries? I *genuinely* did not understand what people were talking about. Now, I do, that's one of the good things to come out of this.

I'm not glad it happened, but I am glad of some of its consequences.

I go to Maria upset about something, and she makes me draw ten circles.

'Who is right in that centre circle?' she asks, explaining that, for some people, it is just themselves.

'It's me and my daughter', I reply.

'You put boundaries up to protect your energy field,' she explains. 'You have your boundaries, and then you learn to deselect the people or circumstances in your life that are depleting your energy.'

Before this, if I met someone who was in a bad mood, I would have felt the need to chase that mood down, try to jump into that person's mind, worrying at it until it was fixed. Worrying at it as if it was mine, when it wasn't. Now, I let it be, let *them* be. Stand back and watch it pass it by me, untouched.

When things fall apart, you don't have a choice but to have boundaries. When it's taking everything you have just to hold things together, then you do not give a minute's thought to saying, 'No, that is too much. I can't take that on/tolerate that behaviour/accomplish that task.' Whereas before you would have said 'Yes, no problem. Give me that plate and I'll just throw it up there with the other thirty I'm currently spinning.' It takes nothing out of you now to say, 'No, I've reached my limit. Sorry, can't, won't, stop, don't.'

Your mental energy, such as you have, is otherwise engaged. You don't have the time to wonder about how others will take it. You do what you need to do. At first, it isn't so much the act of a person who is stronger in their sense of themselves, more the act of someone who is at their limits and simply can't.

But, over time, it can become the former.

Chapter 34

The Crystal Crew

It had been a rough month. I felt like I had been running late from one thing to another, barely keeping my head above water and that there had been no time for anything but getting through. When one of my editors commissioned a piece researching new wellness trends, it was all I could do to stop myself falling on her in gratitude.

My editor is, herself, a former single parent, she has now remarried. 'I know how it feels, you're trying to do everything, while also hanging on by a fine thread,' she said to me once out of the blue as we left a work event, and I felt that rush of comfort you get from someone else seeing, knowing, the reality of your life. Not pity, just *I get it*.

Despite my best efforts, I have let my plan for wellbeing slide, and so I offer myself back up to the world of wellness, a willing guinea pig.

I am like a child in a sweet shop – what to try? How many trends can I cram into my word count?

My research tells me that 'sound baths' are going to be a thing, so I find a woman called Phillipa who is near my house. She has a studio near the Hill of Tara but there isn't time to get down there – this wellness has to be crammed in between school hours and work deadlines. She also sees clients in her flat, so I go down to her. When I arrive, her little son hovers behind her – 'He's home for the day, sick,' she explains matter of factly. I love when women don't feel they need to hide the mothering part of themselves when they are in the professional part of their lives.

She brings me into a bedroom where a huge gong towers between us and the bed. After a short chat, she tells me to lie on the bed. I don't say much but she divines immediately from what I do say that I am practically vibrating with the stress, and that I am in some sort of fear spiral. Unspecified, generalised, fear. A never-ending loop of scenarios going around my mind that terrify. *How will I manage our steep wooden stairs on my own when I am older/what about my pension/journalism is coming to an end/should I get a nine-to-five job/the terror of losing my dream job/and the flexibility with my child it allows for/is my child OK?/exhausted, exhausted, EXHAUSTED.*

'It can feel a bit disorientating,' she says beforehand. 'Or you may just fall deeply asleep, sometimes people do when life is particularly overwhelming.'

I almost instantly fall asleep.

I arrived at her house in a state of high stress, and came out floating. Phillipa tells me that I am safe. That I have nothing to fear, and that I need to keep telling myself that.

She says that I need to tend to 'the vibration at which I am operating', using the words of her technique; this is a sound bath after all. Not to lower it for others or in response to them, but, instead, to look inwards at how I am feeling when I am dealing with something, or someone, difficult. To focus on my own vibration. *When they go low, we go high,* I think.

She tells me that I could operate at a frequency of around eighty, which sounds promising, although I wonder if she's deploying the same technique as Helen the counsellor sometimes does. 'You're clearly flourishing,' she says at the sight of me when I've come from a work event, done up and wearing actual clothes rather than my work-from-home uniform of gym gear or the just-short-of-pyjamas clothes that would be flattering to term 'loungewear'.

'I know what you're at,' I tell her, adding that I have clocked how she always likes to end a session on a positive note, never interrupts me when I'm in the middle of difficult stuff just because my time is up. 'You're trying to make me think I can handle all this, that I am handling all this. Like some sort of self-fulfilling prophecy. I'm onto your strategy.' Helen smiles.

What Phillipa says is similar to what Helen has told me – look inwards to see how you are feeling, rather than worrying about how someone else is. This is usually my barometer for taking a wellness practitioner seriously – has Helen, or my cousin-the-psychologist, said something similar?

I go for reiki, another trend, and while the practitioner works over me, the image of a glass of water, full of sand which is slowly settling, appears in my mind. Afterwards she tells me she spent most of the hour working on my solar-plexus chakra, that she was pulling my reluctant self to the ground. That I am totally ungrounded. It is the fear. I am stuck in fight-or-flight mode, it would seem. I picture one of those stretchy toys my daughter got in a party bag, that you throw on a window and they stick. They can be pulled and pulled and pulled but don't snap.

It's easy to knock the wellness world. So much to mock. So many expensive toys and unfounded medical claims. But also, so much beyond that. People and practices, who will administer advice, or pull you back down, when you cannot do it for yourself. It's not all eggs for your vagina. Unless you have found yourself off kilter, lost on your own trauma map, and in need of finding your way back, probably best not to knock it, or at least that part of it.

Before I start writing my piece, I see a post on Instagram about a new event that is happening during the week, Soul Society. Crystals and guided meditation, run by Merle and Dawn. I decide I can cram in one more trend.

I know nothing of crystals. Merle is a jewellery designer who came to them when she found she had lost her intuition, after becoming a mother. She talks about crystals as if they are talismans and describes how they helped her get back to meditation. She also makes the best homemade doughnuts, which we eat at the break.

I hear this all the time from women I interview for articles or my podcast – the importance of their intuition. They talk about the times when they lost it, that this was a sign that they had sort of lost their way in life, or lost sight of themselves.

Soul Society is held in a small building in Herbert Park. It is deep winter but, as I walk through the park, there are children in shorts playing tennis. *So hardy* I think, and immediately feel guilty that I would never bring my daughter to do such a thing. *Should I be making her hardier?* I wonder. *Am I failing her?* And then immediately dismiss the thought. We're fine. And I can think of nothing worse than shorts in the freezing cold.

As I approach the building, the curtains are open on the full-length glass doors, and I can see the silhouettes of women passing back and forth. The door opens and there stands a small figure with long dark hair and a huge smile. Merle.

'Crystals radiate a calming presence,' she says, as we all sit on our yoga mats around her and Dawn. You *radiate a calming presence*, I think. She compares crystals to physical mantras – assign them meanings, leave them dotted about your house and a glance will remind you what they stand for. Reminders of intentions.

Dawn leads the group in two guided meditations, they are so relaxing that I struggle to stay awake, a worry, I talk in my sleep. Dawn has perfect Meg-Ryan-in-the-eighties hair, runs an online bookstore and is a single mum. Both women are mothers of one. Both are flourishing, and just the sight of them makes me feel better about my own situation. When you see even a glimmer of a reflection of yourself in someone else, and that person seems to be happy and coping and calm, even some of the time, it gives you hope that you too will get there.

Merle needs a guinea pig for a crystal-healing course, and I offer myself up. She arrives at the house and I swear I can feel her calmness emanating at me before I even open the door. She sets up her table – a large, padded bed she has inherited from her mother, a reiki teacher. In the middle of all this, my own mother arrives, dropping in unannounced for a cup of tea.

'Oh!' she says at the sight of us, and I can see her determining to take whatever this is in her stride, trying to keep her face neutral.

'Just a bit of crystal healing,' I carol.

After my mother leaves, I get on the bed, lie down and close my eyes.

'Something might come into your mind, a thought or a message,' Merle says before she begins the guided meditation. 'Something that makes sense.'

I drift in and out, her voice lulls me into a calm I haven't felt in weeks. Life has felt relentless, all bills-to-be-paid and deadlines-to-be-met. My daughter has been sick. Lots of fear, and very little energy with which to fend it off. I feel compressed by it all.

'Anything come to you?' Merle asks as she packs up her treatment table.

'Just think of today,' I say. It popped up out of nowhere, clear as a bell.

Afterwards, we sit over tea and cake, the two of us hiding for an afternoon from our responsibilities. Merle admits to her own struggles with the stresses of motherhood, and coming from someone who outwardly seems so calm, it is additionally comforting.

The following month, I see her again at the next Soul Society. As I gather my yoga mat to leave and grab one of her homemade doughnuts for my daughter, she passes a box into my hand. Inside is a delicate gold chain that has a symbol I have never seen before on it. She has created it out of the letters of 'today', she smiles. 'To remind you,' she says, 'to just think of the day in hand, when it all gets too much.'

Chapter 35

Safe Space

Phillipa is right. Feeling safe is a problem for me. When my husband first moved out, I stopped opening the window in my bedroom at night even though the room then felt uncomfortably warm – it no longer felt safe to fall asleep with an open window. I worried I might wake up to find an intruder in the house.

An angry reader somehow gets my email address and for several days sends aggressive messages about a nothing phrase I used in an article. I sit on my couch and his furious missives land right in the palm of my hand, on my phone.

'Stop checking,' a friend says, but I feel I need to monitor exactly where his rage is at. Has it escalated? How scary is it now? I'm alone and there is no one to distract me, to help me feel safe.

In the aftermath, you need to find a new safe space – or spaces, ideally. You spread yourself around, rather than place it all in one person. The person you live with is a child, you are their safe space. They cannot be yours. Happy place, yes. Safe space, no.

I have one sibling, a younger brother. There is four years between us, so there was never any jealousy on my part when he arrived. At times, he was MY baby, and I would insist on feeding him, torturous, no doubt, for my mother. Growing up, I was in charge. I still remember the moment he realised that he did not, in fact, *have* to obey my every command. I was fifteen and he was eleven. Stretched out on our living-room couch, I drawled carelessly 'Make us a cup of tea, Dar?' Almost reflexively he got up to go to the kitchen, then paused at the door. I could see it dawning across his face, the knowledge that he did not have to make me a cup of tea. 'No,' he declared triumphantly and, just like that, my power slipped away throughout my hands.

For several years, my brother lived in China, studying. Every September, before he returned after a summer at home, we would all say goodbye at my parents' house after a family lunch. I would always cry in a manner that seemed a bit overdramatic given that I was a thirty-something-year-old woman. We're not effusive in our family and, really, I was embarrassing myself as much everyone else with my dramatics.

But I couldn't help it.

Even though I am the older sibling by four years, I wanted to lie on the ground and cling to his ankles. Beg him not to go. Thankfully, I spared us all that embarrassment. At the start of each summer when we would go to the airport to meet him, I would cry again, walking slightly ahead of the rest of them towards the car, mortified, but overcome by a wave of relief.

At the time, I didn't really understand where this uncontrollable sobbing came from. Now, I think that, deep down within me, I knew that there were cracks within my own world. My brother provided a sense of safety and I hated seeing him go.

When my daughter was one, he came home from China for the summer with his girlfriend, Song Yue.

My parents had gone on holiday and I was piecemealing together childcare for my daughter with various family members. Daragh hadn't seen his niece in ten months, Song Yue had never met her. Right then, that didn't matter, there was a work event I had to be at and I desperately need their help. *You may cry all day,* I think, anticipating her reaction at being left with utter strangers, *but at least I know you are safe and with people who love you.*

They are barely in the door when I start throwing instructions about bottles, nappies and nap times at them. 'She probably won't sleep for you, so don't worry about it,' I say over my shoulder, running out the door.

When I get home that evening, Daragh and Song Yue looked exhausted, my daughter blissfully happy, cooing in Song Yue's arms, looking up at her adoringly with a toothless grin. She was not a child who would go to just anyone back then.

But she has gone straight into the arms of these two.

Now, I have gone into a work tunnel in which, from the moment I get back from the playschool run to late at night, I am at my desk (dining table), working on a big project, an end-of-week deadline looming. My brother comes and takes over on the domestic front. He makes us spaghetti Bolognese exactly as we like it (by which I mean how the four-year-old likes it – I would happily consume any food prepared and cooked for me by another).

He knows exactly how finely to cut up her pasta, how thinly the vegetables need to be chopped to ensure she cannot see them and will therefore eat them, how to distract her when pre-dinner hunger tends to spill over into meltdown.

'I'm hangry,' she announces, coming to stand by my elbow, and I wonder, not for the first time, why on *earth* I taught her that word.

He knows what temperature her bath needs to be, where the towels are kept and the order of proceedings for getting her out (plug out, she stands up, lift over side, towel quick as you can, lift out of bathroom to avoid cold tiles, make it to couch, few minutes of toonies).

I don't have to tell him where her pyjamas are or how to hang the blackout blind exactly right so light won't creep in around its edges and wake her earlier than seven. He has even sourced a specific track on iTunes she likes to fall asleep to.

I do not need to tell him anything, he just steps in and does it.

Another day, he lets her help him while he installs my new internet router, just like my mother let me help her by feeding him all those years ago.

At bedtime, my daughter has forgotten to bring up her new favourite toy – he knows what it is and where it is, and he brings it up to us so we do not have to leave the bed we are now settled into. 'Uncle Dar-y', my daughter coos. And I am still, at times, invisibly clinging to him for safety.

I install an alarm, and I hear my neighbours pottering, and as time passes, there is nowhere I feel safer than in our cosy home.

Chapter 36

Book Club

Stand beside me for long enough and I will form a club around us. It's almost a compulsion. 'I'm going to start a supper club,' I announced to Sophie.

'What, and *charge* people?' she replied.

There followed several minutes of talking at cross purposes before her brow cleared and she said, 'Aaaaah, you mean like an English dinner party? Where people don't know each other?'

I realise that actually this is beginning to sound like too much hassle, given my limited cooking skills. I decide instead upon a book club.

I grew up faintly aware of my mother's monthly book-club meetings – all Cork women, some she has known since they were teenagers. These get-togethers, from my vantage point of peering in from the kitchen door, seemed to be less about books, more about that kind of half-shouting-half-crying-with-laughter communication only a group of women can do together.

Now, from what I can tell, even the pretence of a book being read has been almost entirely discarded and they are a go-away-on-weekends-together club. It had always seemed like a particularly fun way to spend an evening. I tried and failed to set one up in my twenties, aspirations quashed when one friend told me disgustedly that she was far too young to be in a book club.

Some months after the separation, my friend Aisling asks me to be in a book club with some women from work. The same week, my cousin asks me to be in another, with a group of women I don't know. Soon after, I decide to form a third. Again it's like being at a pick 'n' mix.

I ask fourteen women, because people always drop out.

The first meeting is at my house. It's a Friday night, the rain is coming down in sheets, and I have left it until the last minute to go to Lidl for supplies. By the time I am home and doing a last-minute tidy, I've whipped myself into a perfect storm of feeling sorry for myself. Imagining all the others leaving cosy houses with husbands to come to my book club. Which is ridiculous and not even the case.

Then the women arrive, and they make themselves at home instantly, in the way the best guests do. Spreading out, getting stuck in, not waiting to be asked. We have decided we will do tapas, so everyone brings something. Esther is in the kitchen, she has brought a plant as a gift and is making her signature guacamole. Soobie is piling a veritable leaning tower of dips on the counter – my daughter and I will dine for days afterwards on various flavours of hummous. Elle and Rachel sit on the couch frantically trying to finish the book. Merle has made Bounty bars. Not everyone makes it that night (standard book-club etiquette and why it is best to invite more people than you think you will need). Not everyone has read the book (standard etiquette for our book club). Sophie stages a dramatic re-enactment of the book for those who haven't finished it.

I look around at this circle of women sitting in my living room. Some of them are meeting for the first time. I am the only one who knows all of them. And because of this, I know that each of them is, or has had to, contend with something. It makes me feel a little less alone.

I do not think it is just me, who in the aftermath of a marriage breakdown feels the need for clubs of women. It feels like this is a time of women clubbing together.

Chapter 37

The Coping Class

Sophie and I spend many Saturday afternoons on the couch at one of our houses while the children play around us. In the middle of one of our hours-long conversations, I mention the idea of a book or some kind of series, interviewing women who have gone through something difficult, about how they coped. Like all her family, Sophie is a natural editor. 'That would make a good podcast,' she says immediately, and, before I know it, I have emailed Cassie, who produces and hosts podcasts with Sophie, and pitched the idea to her. Just three interviews into recording *How To Fall Apart*, something becomes blindingly obvious. Coping can be a trap.

We wear our ability to cope as a badge of honour.

'Yes, things are awful, but just look at me coping. Look. Look at how I am managing it all; shouldering burdens, keeping going.' It's like a new form of the busyness brag. Something we brag about which isn't really doing us much good.

'My life may be falling apart, but I can manaaaaaaage.'

'Things may be bad for me right now, but I am so strong, so still in some sort of control.'

And then we cope ourselves into a corner, and it becomes too shameful and too scary to admit that, actually, right now, we may not be coping. Because we've kept ourselves going with the thought of the sheer impressiveness of our ability to cope.

Or it's too inconvenient to stop coping. If you are working and mothering or caring for others – older parents, an unwell spouse – where the hell do you find the time and life space to fall apart, even on a small scale?

Which is the next problem.

What if it is not on a small scale?

Helen tells me that buried trauma needs to released carefully, ideally with the help of a professional, so that it does not overwhelm us. But what if everything we have been pressing down explodes all over our lives? What if we can't release it in small, managed doses?

What if we stop coping and let it out – and it breaks us all over again? Can we take that risk?

My friend Kate talked about it in the book she

wrote about her own divorce, *Untying the Knot*. How she got through the hardest parts and then sitting on the beach one day watching her children play, the sun on her back, the worst apparently over, she was hit by a panic attack. I remember Kate's experience when I'm sitting in the park one day with Lewine, chatting as our children run about us. Out of nowhere, I feel a wave of unease rise up and wash over me. I cannot shake it off; horrible anxiety laced with dread. A vice-like knot tightening in my stomach. I take shallow breaths because I don't seem to be able to breathe properly. It felt like watching my life while I was trapped inside a glass bubble of fear. I said nothing, hoping that, by not naming it, it would go away.

I drop my daughter to my father, tell him 'I think I'm having a p-a-n-i-c a-t-t-a-c-k,' not wanting her to know.

I couldn't shake it – deep breathing, meditating, walking into town where I had to go for a work event later, none of it worked. I told myself that, if this becomes a regular thing, I am going to the doctor and demanding Valium or whatever is necessary.

The next day, after it has passed, feels like I'm walking across frozen water that could crack at any minute, plunging me back in.

I don't trust the calm.

Chapter 38

The Life Partner

Rachel and I lived together in our twenties, long before there were husbands or marriages. We met when Nancy, a mutual friend who was moving to London, set up a sort of friend date, because she knew we would take to each other. We did.

We were both looking for somewhere new to live, so quickly joined forces, and found somewhere together.

We were both at that point in your early twenties where you have left college and are floundering frantically – desperate to start the next part of our lives, but with no idea what to do.

On nights out, we were often asked if we were sisters or life partners – that we were friends never seemed to occur to people. We took the term to heart and adopted it for ourselves – we have been LPs ever since.

If she is your friend, Rachel is both the fiercest and gentlest on-your-team person I know. Always ready to get in high indignation on your behalf. But simultaneously grievously hurt for you. Throughout the worst of things, she would text me regularly to check in and I would fail to respond for weeks and then ring out of the blue, crying, and she would drop everything to listen and console. Or we would go for a walk, which would often no get further than us sitting in the car park at the beach, me sobbing, her listening.

On one occasion, halfway through a phone call, it transpired that she was at the park with her partner and their baby. When I rang, she had answered immediately and then silently directed them to the café and walked off to talk to me, letting me know none of this, until I asked about their whereabouts. She has seen me through all of this, known what was happening as it happened. It's a gift, being burdenless; friends who do not require explanations, who do not quibble when you disappear for weeks or months.

Rachel invites me to a birthday party; Mags, a friend of hers whom I have never met, is turning fifty.

'But I don't know her. Won't it be odd?' I quibble.

'Not at all,' she says firmly. 'She told me to bring someone.'

'She probably meant your partner, but OK,' I huff churlishly.

She assures me that she didn't and in the spirit of

welcoming in the new, I go, even though I am slightly mortified at what I deem to be gate-crashing this event.

'I'm going to a party with a friend,' I tell another friend, who is also separated. 'I won't know anyone there, I don't really want to go, but I feel I should. I'm sure I'll enjoy it.'

'You'll possibly hate it, but you have to go anyway,' she replies.

And then I meet Mags, and she welcomes me as if she could not be more delighted to meet me, had in fact been particularly expecting me, and I realise she is one of life's natural network builders, a connector. Rach and I sit out on the balcony looking over Dublin Bay, drinking prosecco and eating 99s, and it is lovely.

At dinner, I am sat next to a woman who has been separated for years – I am a veritable diviner. She tells me about her lovely stepson and her lovely life, and I know that it's all a way of her kindly, subtly reassuring me that things will all be OK in the end. I feel she can read the shellshock on my face as I can spot on other women who are going through something. If you know, you know. When you plug yourself into the matrix of women, you find similar stories everywhere you go.

Also at our table is Ellie Kisyombe. She, along with several of the other women at the party, are all members of a supper club that Mags formed. She had pulled together a number of her female friends to meet regularly at each other's houses for a dinner and a catch-up, because catching up with each one individually doesn't always happen and she wanted to make sure she saw them without months going by between each meeting.

The other women didn't know each other, but now they are all friends, and they go away together. They have each other to their homes, except for Ellie. Ellie is possibly the best cook in the group, an actual professional, but she lives in Direct Provision, so she doesn't have a table of her own at which to host her friends, no home to invite her gang to. The others lend her theirs, she tells me. Mags stores her stuff in her garage.

I ask Ellie if she will do an interview with me. She tells me how she was ousted from the apartment she had lived in within Direct Provision for several years, where she had made a home for her family; she and her teenage twins. Where there was a kitchen, and room for each of them to have a space of their own. A letter arrived out of the blue, telling her they were moving to the commuter belt, to a town where she and her twins know no one.

Eventually, after months of resistance, she was moved to another centre, nearer to Dublin, but a place she says is the worst of everywhere she has stayed since she went into the system years before.

'How do you cope with the stress? I asked her.

Because Ellie does not seem like someone who is being broken by the system within which she is forced to live. By this life over which, at that time, she has so little control. She seems to me to be a person who can still be joyful.

'I have a lot of friends and people in my life,' Ellie replies. 'But I also spend a lot of time on my own. And no one really knows this but, when I am on my own, I cry a lot.'

It sounds bleak, but what she's doing is actually a good thing. What the outside world might consider a person falling apart, is actually someone coping. Sometimes coping is just sitting still and letting it all out. Instead of numbing herself, she was at least acknowledging the pain she was feeling, an emotional pain that, at times, she tells me takes on a physical aspect. She felt pain in her body from the stress and trauma. Ellie is brave for facing it, rather than pushing it down and ignoring it.

*

Several weeks later, I am sitting in front of my computer at our dining-room table, and I look down to discover tears splashing on my hands. I hadn't even noticed I was crying. I remember Ellie's words. I have been so immobilised by stress, that all I can do is sit and cry.

Chapter 39

In Which I am Broken by the Animal Kingdom

I had decided to get a dog – a decision which turned out to be an act of self-delusion of gargantuan proportions. For starters, I am a lapsed cat person, not a dog person. I'm not sure I even really like dogs. As a child, I was quite scared of them.

I see now that I was trying to prove that this matter of a marital breakdown wasn't going to stop me in any way doing whatever I wanted. Ridiculous, in hindsight, especially given that, if we hadn't separated, there is no way I would have contemplated a dog.

I comforted myself with visions of dog and daughter rolling about the place together, and ignored the fact that I am practically phobic about dog poo. On our walks to the park, my daughter scoots ahead, shouting gleefully 'DOG POO MOMMY' every few seconds, knowing my vigilance for spotting and reacting in horror to the stuff.

But no. I had a point to prove. Separation? No problem. What you can do, we can do.

And so, I ignored the fact that life was only of late coming to a place that felt manageable for significant stretches of time. And that this was a situation that in no way equated to having room in my life for taking on the minding of another small creature who is not toilet trained, will not sleep through the night, cannot even travel in a car without becoming quite hysterical, and was going to cost a ton of money.

'Should I have another child?' I had asked Helen the counsellor in a moment of guilt-ridden madness. One of the lesser-known benefits of separating is that if you are a parent of one, people finally stop telling you you couldn't possibly dream of allowing them to be an only child, as if this was one of the worst fates imaginable.

'Let's ignore the practicalities of making that happen for a moment and just tell me what you picture when you think of that,' Helen said to my suggestion.

I answer immediately. 'It's two in the morning. I'm standing alone in my living room, a baby in my arms. It won't sleep, it's screaming. My daughter is sitting on the stairs, crying. I'm wearing the once-blue-now-grey dressing gown, not sure when I last showered. I too am crying. We're all crying.'

'I think that answers that question,' Helen replied briskly.

I ignored the gentle questioning of my family at the dog plan, which I knew was really an attempt to say as politely as possible, 'What on *earth* are you thinking?'

It is testament to how much people will let you off the hook during a divorce that they barely allowed a trace of *what the hell are you thinking* into their demeanour.

Sophie questioned it repeatedly, 'So, you're really getting one? A dog?'

Lewine ignored it when I mentioned it in our group WhatsApp.

I knew what both were getting at. I ignored them.

Ignored the scepticism of my ex, who had actually had a dog, so really did know what he was talking about. Ignored is probably the wrong word. Treated his doubt as a bull would a red rag. Became more determined, obviously. *Of course I can do this.*

This dog was a badge of coping. *Nothing to see here world, we are FIIIIIIIINNNNEE. If we want to take on a dog, we will do it. We have in no way been constrained by our circumstances.*

Bringing home an actual live creature. *What was I thinking?*

I had searched for the right dog for months, and barely noticed the parameters of my requirements changing. My red lines – no puppies, must be small, must be trained – disappeared one by one until we were bringing home an entirely untrained Lurcher pup.

'How big will it eventually grow?' my mother asked doubtfully, looking around our two-bedroom terrace.

'They have no idea,' I snapped. 'Impossible to say.' Ignoring all evidence to the contrary of every other Lurcher since the beginning of time.

The dog had only been home with us two hours when I rang the rescue centre. 'We need more help,' I whimpered plaintively down the phone. I was out in the garden, whispering in the hope that the others wouldn't overhear this admission of defeat. 'I have no idea what I'm doing here, and she keeps getting excited and running laps around the living room and if my daughter is sitting on the couch she sort of runs over her. Please send help.'

It was Sunday. The next day, help arrived, in the form of a dog trainer who tells me that she still wouldn't leave her three-year-old niece alone with her own dog – an eight-year-old, trained by her, a professional – for a minute.

'Great. Why did none of you point that out?' I want to scream.

We had just got to the point of independent play. Only the week previous, I had sat on the couch and read – *read* – for an hour, Van Morrison playing in the background, my daughter on the floor beside me, playing with her dolls house, and it had felt like everything would be OK. And now there is talk of reinstating downstairs baby gates, and I have to take my child with me to the bathroom whenever I go, because it is not safe to leave her alone with the puppy.

There follows several days of intense stress. As puppies go, from what I can gather, Ruby is quite calm. But she cannot be left alone in a room with my daughter. 'C'mon, Bean, we're going to the bathroom again,' I say, and we trudge off together, herself baffled.

In the afternoon while making dinner one day, I have to trap my daughter upstairs, locking the remaining stair gate I have yet to get around to dismantling. Each morning, she calls for me to help her get dressed, while the dog wails downstairs to be let out. I rush between the two, satisfying no one. The second night, I lay in bed sobbing to myself. 'What have you done? You loved your life.' I thought back longingly to only two days ago, when it was me and her, and I didn't have to clean shit from my back garden every day. I cry in frustration at having thrown away the relative ease that we had come to know. At the realisation of how much easier things had become, only for me to have thrown it all away.

I have never felt more single-parentish than when we got the dog, this unmanageable project I had foisted upon myself as my ex, parents and best friends looked on askance.

It took me a while to call myself a single-parent – probably because of the shame or horror at finding myself the I-don't-know-how-she-does-it-woman – and then I did a deep dive and used the phrase constantly. If you find yourself being stigmatised, sometimes you want to take it on and shout it from the roof tops. I'm so supported and such a co-parent that I'm sometimes not sure if the term is accurate. I don't feel very single. But then I think I'll call myself what I like. A single mother.

The dog is another matter. Mine alone.

I am utterly on my own with this one, and I resent almost instantly her encroachment on the lovely little unit of two we have built up. We go for an evening walk, my daughter enjoying liberally scattering the dog food we've been told to use to keep her from wandering, and I plod bitterly behind them, glaring at the dog, intruding on our little unit.

Everyone loves her, she is a particularly pretty dog, it seems, and I do enjoy our walks during the day, chatting to other dog owners – a group I now, to my surprise, find myself a part of. How she sits quietly in her basket while I work. *Maybe in a few years, Ruby*, I think guiltily. *But right now, I have all I can handle.*

Midweek, Sophie announces she is dropping over. I think she has sensed an escalating horror in the tone of my voice throughout the week. When the dog does her hourly routine of growl, crouch, sharp barking then scramble around the room, over the couch and whoever happens to be on it, she takes it all in. Me, with absolutely no idea what I am doing and no clue how to make her stop or calm her down, shuffling nervously about the place. I'm scared of her, if I'm honest, when that barking starts. I feel utterly at sea, skittishly trying to settle her while she nips at my fingers.

'Grief makes a person do strange things,' Sophie says kindly but firmly, as I watch on impressed that she barely seems to notice the nipping of her fingers I've been told is normal for a pup. 'We'll put it down to that.'

The next day, my mother and I go back to the rescue centre.

'Is she here to see the vet?' the man who had originally helped us says warmly, leaning down to stroke Ruby.

'No, she has to come back. It's not working.'

He drops her paw like something diseased, gives me a look of disgusted horror and turns on his heel. It is too much; already a woman on the edge, I burst into tears at this failed dog-owner-shaming.

'Is it the thought of letting her go?' the co-worker who replaces him asks sympathetically at the sight of my upset, and I nod silently, letting her believe that.

Although she seems nonplussed by the whole thing, I worry about the upset it may cause my daughter, instantly guiltly promise a L.O.L. doll.

Weeks later, my daughter shouts across the aisle in Aldi, 'Mommy, we need this food for our dog.'

Here it is, I think. Proof that I have broken her. Here is the evidence, the extreme denial finally shattering. What is to come?

'We don't have a dog, sweetheart,' I say gingerly. 'Remember, she went back?'

'My future dog mum,' she says with an almost full-body eye roll. The relief is overwhelming.

Chapter 40

The Perimeter is Breached

Unfortunately, our encounters with the animal kingdom are not over. Still slightly high on the stress of that week, ten days later, I look up from the couch where I am working late one evening to see a rodent scurrying out of the kitchen. It stops, looks at me. I look at it.

At least, this is how I now remember it. The next thing I know I am across the room slamming the door at the now retreating creature, and then I'm back on the couch, only now I'm perched on the arm, the highest place I can get to.

Regression kicks in immediately. I think I've done fairly well so far on the living without another adult front, but I have been vanquished by animals. Just a week earlier, I had caught a huge spider under a glass and, in between Googling the existence of False Widows in Ireland, called my brother for him to come over and eject it from the house.

You really learn what you are made of when a small animal invades your home. I, it transpires, am made of the kind of stuff that screams, jumps to the highest available spot and calls her dad. It is eleven o'clock but he answers and says he's on his way. I spend the ten minutes until his arrival Googling differences between a rat and a mouse.

A search of the premises unearths no evidence that the intruder is still among us. 'Want to come to our house for the rest of the night?' my father asks. I consider momentarily, but still nothing trumps the primacy of my personal dictum; never wake a sleeping child, especially one for whom it takes an hour to get to sleep in the first place. I watch him block up the small space under the kitchen door with tissue paper, horrified by visions of boneless creatures oozing their way out in the middle of the night to come and crawl all over me and my daughter. Needless to say, I don't sleep.

'It didn't have the innately evil demeanour you would associate with a rat,' I tell Sophie on the phone the next morning as I wait for Rentokil to arrive. 'It wasn't black or the size of a rabbit or with an obscenely large tail,' I continue. You take your comforts where you can. Not rabbit-sized.

But I know, and my fears are confirmed when I watch the professional do a little jump back in horror when he finds the point at which, hidden behind the kitchen presses, it had found entry.

'Oh that's a rat all right,' he says, and I want to sink

to the floor and just lie there, give up. Instead, I pack up our things and temporarily move home to my parents' house, where I sit on the couch, stunned, watching in a daze as my parents, brother and sister-in-law-to-be move about me, minding my daughter, leaving me to it.

It being my internal falling apart. I have discovered my breaking point.

'Finding a rat in your house is far more stressful than divorce,' I take to telling people afterwards. Which is nonsense, of course. It's just an easier stress to admit, for being that bit more manageable a situation.

After my brother and father block up the entry hole (concrete mixed with glass – rats are chewers, the Rentokil man tells me and I can barely restrain from wailing *the horror*), I stand in the kitchen, ready to embark on the great clean up. I've watched Mrs Hinch; I have a collection of bottles of Zoflora.

But I'm frozen. Rooted to the spot. I cannot come up with the next step. Where to even begin?

Our home has been a haven, and now it is a place of intense stress, a rat ready to jump out from behind every corner. It's too much for me. There is nowhere that is not stressful. My whole life a place of fight or flight.

I am immobilised by stress.

'Just throw it all out,' I think. 'Start again.'

I do it – and it is strangely cathartic. My phone dies, and I've no idea where my charger is and I just leave it. This never happens.

I step out of life for a few hours, and clean that kitchen to within an inch of its life. Mindfulness courtesy of a rodent. Surprisingly effective.

Chapter 41

The Runaways

My daughter and I run away to Shereen and her daughters, who are living temporarily in the countryside, at her older sister Naadia's house. At school, her sister was quite simply the coolest person we knew. On Saturdays, we would trawl through shops in Temple Bar to find similar dyed-purple Levi flares. She wore hers with a bright-red jumper, a colour combination that, to my teenager eyes, seemed nothing short of revolutionary. She is now a doctor and a mother of four, and since my daughter has been a baby I have rung her on occasion with queries from 'Can she sleep in the bed?', to 'There's a slim chance she has an ear infection and we're flying tomorrow'. She is always calming. Now her house by the sea offers a much-needed bolthole.

From the outside, our trip doesn't suggest anything like the drama of a running away. Single mothers who are self-employed don't up and leave unplanned in dramatic fashion. The trip has, in fact, been planned for weeks. They are living out west and we are going to visit. But as everything is feeling a bit much, it feels satisfyingly like we are escaping it all.

My daughter and Shereen's eldest get on brilliantly. 'She's my best friend, Mummy,' her daughter says in a London accent that, to me, sounds like something out of *Oliver*. It soothes my addledness to hear the child of my oldest friend loving mine. We go to the beach, Silverstrand, 'The mermaid Mommy!' shouts my daughter, a Julia Donaldson fan, and we look out for one.

The girls carry buckets, collect stones, are nearly blown over in the wind, and eat rice cakes and crisps. Back at the house, we let them watch endless episodes of *Trolls* as we hide out on the balcony and look at the sea. I tell her everything. How it gets much easier, and then much harder. The grind that feels relentless at times. When the children are in bed, I work and Shereen listens to podcasts, our silence is easy and companionable. It feels nice to be living with another adult for a few days. Discussing what we'll have for dinner, getting the children ready for bed together, having a glass of wine after they are asleep.

Chapter 42
Spa Nights

Back home, I instigate spa nights, after I have invented them. For evenings when I am exhausted, but am trying not to turn on the TV. Spa nights can constitute anything from painting our nails, to my daughter lying on my bed while I rub her back gently with my nails. On one spa night, Grandad is recruited; they pile up pillows and cushions on her bed and he reads to her while she chomps on strawberries. I lie next door on my bed, too tired to do anything but stare at the ceiling.

Chapter 43

The Broken Home

I first started looking for a house to buy when I was twenty-six, just before I met my husband. I had fallen into my dream career of journalism in my very early twenties, when most of my friends were still trying to figure out just what theirs might be, so I was ahead of the curve on that one; the first by a long shot to buy.

What I wanted, I decided, was something bijou, near town – and I found it. A two-up two-down near the sea, five minutes from my family home, and close enough to work and the city centre for me to walk. It is now covered in a wisteria I planted almost ten years ago, which has yet to throw up any actual flowers.

A starter home, maybe an investment property that I would keep to rent rather than sell when I inevitably moved on. Don't judge me, it was 2007, we were all property investors then.

My mother came with me to the first viewing and, every time the estate agent turned her back, we would look at each other and silent scream in excitement. In perfect condition – the seller had set the table with new crockery, bought new beds and dressed the tables beside with copies of Maeve Binchy and Marian Keyes boks – we knew immediately this was the one.

After the split, there was no moving for me and my daughter. But even though our address stayed the same, we still had to set up a new home. A reconfiguration. I come across a book by Deborah Levy in which she describes setting up a new home for herself and her daughters after her own divorce. It gets me thinking – nice to embrace the thing.

Is it shallow to admit that a tiny part of me is relishing the freedom of making interiors choices without consulting another? I think again sadly of my collection of John Rocha cushions, boiled wool and metal-embellished, aesthetically pleasing but admittedly not comfortable, which I agreed to get rid of after we moved in.

Several months after my husband moves out I start on a redecorating kick with something of a passion. It's low-effort stuff. The odd new cushion, a few vases. No surface is safe from being liberally draped in fairy lights. I move the bed around. *My* bed, now.

I put one of the bedside tables into my daughter's room and it feels like a big move, a sort of statement of no return.

There's a house beside where we get our Friday curry that has a pink door and, each time we pass it, we debate whether or not we will paint our own a similar shade. A declaration that we are a now a house of women.

I install the Photobox app and, having barely printed off a picture since my daughter's birth, order her lifetime's worth. Our life in polaroid jumps out at us from every surface of the house, cheering us on. 'Look how much joy there has been – there is – despite it all. You can do this.'

For my first birthday after my husband moved out, in lieu of a gift, I ask my father and my brother to put together a new bedroom dresser I have bought. Hemnes, eight-drawer – your classic IKEA. Probably feeling sorry for me, in a moment of weakness which I suspect they came to regret almost immediately, they agreed. Or maybe I just had a clearer idea of what they were in for than they did. Between the collecting, the building, the ancillary trips to the hardware store to purchase the it-turns-out not included dowels, and the involvement of my determined-to-help three-and-three-quarter-year-old (her specificity, not mine), the whole thing takes three days. Throughout, they kindly assure me they are not hating life, or me, a kindness that is a gift in itself.

My father is exactly like his own father, an engineer who would take apart and put back together entire cars with his brother on a Sunday for fun, and who would patiently explain the workings of things to us, his small grandchildren, treating us with a patience he did not always choose to display in his dealings with adults.

Her grandfather's encouragement goes to my daughter's head and she takes to banging random surfaces with her small hammer. When I object, she tells me sternly, 'But I'm *very* good at hammering', with the self-satisfaction only a small child can muster. The one begetting the other (talent with hammer equals hitting things, obviously) so self-explanatory she can't quite believe I need to have this explained.

'You're battening down the hatches', a friend says. But it's not that, actually it's the opposite. The storm has passed – or is passing; we're at the tail end. If anything, the hatches are being uncovered, because the danger of capsizing has retreated. It feels more like nesting. Me with my fairy lights and pictures of everyone we love; my daughter with her hammer. We are building a new nest for ourselves.

I Google 'nesting after separation' out of curiosity, expecting lots of Mumsnet threads. It turns out it is an actual strategy of co-parenting after a break-up. The children stay in the family home, the parents each have a separate abode and take it in turns to spend a week with the kids.

'It's like something from a teenager's bedroom in here,' a friend says of the new dresser, which I have decorated liberally with lamps, jewellery and make-up. She is right. I remember doing this sort of thing as a young teenager in my parents' house. Staying up into the small hours dragging furniture about the room, changing the layout of Blur, Oasis and dolphin posters, the tower of Coke cans Shereen and I inexplicably began to collect for a time.

Maybe this sort of physical rearrangement of one's space comes with the territory of entering a new phase.

In work, writing for the property pages, I write cover stories about people looking for their forever home. It is usually their second home, the home they will put down roots in, raise their children in, grow old in. They imagine a space that can expand and contract around them, the open-plan kitchen where they will watch their small children, the separate living room to hide from them when they are teenagers. I had always thought I would need a bigger house to contain the life I was planning.

It's a sunny late-autumn afternoon and my daughter and I sit on the step looking out at our garden, wooden doors open, the warmth on our legs, sharing a bowl of strawberries. Van Morrison plays in the background – always our shortcut to a sense of wellbeing.

That evening she is going to her grandparents for a few days and, as my father brings her bag to the car outside, she turns to me. 'I'll miss you and the house, Mommy. I wish you were coming so I would only miss the house.' And it makes absolute sense to me that she would rank our home as a living thing.

When everywhere else requires some level of hitching up of one's defences, home is a place to put it all down, to just be. 'Our house,' my daughter sternly corrects me when she overhears me saying 'my house' to someone.

'Our house, our rules,' I jokingly tell her one day, a variation of her favourite saying, 'my room, my rules'. It's a habit that is good for personal boundaries; bad for playdates.

Her face is awash with delight at the thought that she is an equal ruler in our domain. She never lets me forget I said it.

Now it looks like this will be my forever home. Our two-up two-down wisteria-without-flowers-clad redbrick terrace with my parents nearby, contracting perfectly to fit our new life exactly.

Chapter 44

The Woman Who Didn't Find Balance

For months, I kept bumping into things, knocking my legs or elbows on the open dishwasher door or the doorframe, things I should have easily missed.

It was as if I was slightly off balance from the rest of the world and could not get out of the way of even the obvious obstructions.

I interviewed Dr Rhona Mahony once about a piece on work-life balance. She pops up everywhere in the stories of other women I interview, always vigilant on their behalf. Waiting at the door of Holles Street for a premature labour to arrive in an ambulance. Appearing behind the curtains in a ward of new mothers, knowing somehow that behind the show of togetherness a woman is not OK. Protectively guiding someone who is having her first baby after the loss of a child. I asked her if she had found balance, this mother of four with her huge job and all that dedication. She smiled at me, inclined her head as if to say, *Come on, we both know better than that,* and chuckled softly. Because of course we both knew.

Nobody finds a perfect balance. Men aren't expected to; women are, but don't.

For those first few months after we separated, I struggled to find a balance between my severely depleted energy levels and not spending the weekend lying on the couch watching cartoons, feeling guilty for doing nothing.

All those boxes to be ticked. Child time. Seeing friends. Doing a food shop. Getting some exercise in. Work. All this, accompanied by the background noise of exhaustion. Without the infrastructure of the week to hold me up at the weekend, I realise how shattered I am. It's banal, but there it is; tiredness is the thing I struggle with the most.

Surprisingly, the answer, on those really exhausted weekends, if I didn't want to lie around the house doing nothing with my daughter and then feel bad about it afterwards like I was letting her down – or see the loneliness creep in and regret it – was getting out on pre-planned, full-day outings. Big set pieces, already tested. When you're depleted, it can be hard to come up with something in the moment. Best to rely on things you already know work. And, conversely, when exhausted, getting out can make you forget your tiredness, when staying home would just have served to emphasise it.

These days are for just the two of us because, when you feel a bit raw with exhaustion, it can be easier to focus all your energy on one thing, your child.

One of our favourite outings is a day trip into town. The DART in, Milano's on Dawson Street for pizza, then around the art galleries, most of which have children's workshops at the weekend. Nothing makes you feel more like you're doing OK by your child than doing something a bit arts-and-craftsy with them.

Look at us, no iPad in the hand to see here. We may have separated by but, by God we baked, we glued, we glittered, we read endless books.

If there's time, we go to the Natural History Museum, the dead zoo. To finish up, a trip to Merrion Square's playground, where I will stand below the climbing frame making an idiot of myself shouting up at her, occasionally going up after her because I'm convinced she is about to come tumbling down, or has got stuck in the tower.

Our big day in town is a formula that enables me to feel as if we've cracked weekends. Not yet ready to see how we feel and play it by ear, we have plans to fall back on.

'You're my best friend, Beanie,' I say to her with

a grin, as we leave our favourite cafe where we had stopped for coffee and cake. It's a joke between us. She doesn't know it, but, years earlier, her father and I had a neighbour who used to lament her teenage daughter growing up. 'She used to be my best friend.' It became an in-joke between us, her parents, the best-friend mother. Now it is an in-joke between me and our daughter.

Depending on her mood, she will smile back and say, 'You too, Mommy', or throw me a pitying look and say, 'Roo is my best friend, Mommy.'

Grandad collects us, always from the same spot between the playground and the gallery, which doesn't stop us from jumping up and down wildly when we see his car so he cannot miss us. We drive home in the late-autumn sun, Van Morrison weather.

Chapter 45

Me-time

After my ex had moved into his own place, I had rung my aunt who has worked with organisations that support single parents in a panic one night.

'How will I cope with it?' I sobbed down the phone, the prospect of my daughter staying in a different house suddenly appalling me at one o'clock in the morning.

'The things is,' she told me calmly, 'one of the big problems can be that if a father isn't familiar with the little routines of a child's day – bathtime, bedtime – then children can feel homesick for their mother when they are with him.' She told me this because she knew it wasn't the case for us, that my child would never feel homesick with her father, and so she knew I would be comforted by that thought. She also relayed that, sometimes, fathers spend the night in the home you live in with your child, and you go elsewhere. I might stay at my parents. 'It's a way of easing everyone into things.'

Other people will tell you when you separate that you need to go straight into a clear division, no grey area. Ignore them. You and your ex are the ones who know what works best for your family. Sometimes, there are situations where you do not run gladly towards any of the options. That doesn't mean you do not have to choose one of them. It might not be ideal, but it might also be the best thing for your family at that time. It could be separate lives, or coming and going from the one house. The grey area can be uncomfortable but sometimes it's necessary for a time.

Either way, having another parent who knows all the how-to-get-the-socks-on-without-a-meltdown, or rinse-shampoo-from-the-hair tricks means you can go off without a second glance. Being a single parent means accepting an, at times whiplash, adjustment. The full-on-ness of being the only adult, then suddenly nothing, when your child is with the other parent and you are on your own.

It had been a while since my last wellness-plan macro break. In the day-to-day, I had forgotten about them, those big, dramatic inserts in life that I had planned to try to take every couple of months. In the absence of big nights out, bottles of wine on the couch with a spouse, I had saved for occasional weekends away. When you are going through a crisis, you don't just need the smaller habits that buffer you, you need big, blow-off-steam, pull-you-back-from-the-edge, stuff.

Pressure valves. Things I hoped would ensure I stayed on top of the stress. Or, at the very least, did not combust from it.

I do not, in general, very much care for the bashing on about mothers taking me-time. 'Don't feel guilty for needing time to yourself,' someone bleats at me from an Instagram story, and I think, *Jesus, of course I don't*. It makes such martyrs out of mothers – or 'Mamas', as they are referred to.

There's also the fact that, as I progress further into single motherhood, all this urging woman to take it easy, take a break, seems to come from a place of sometimes blinkered privilege. Lifestyle privilege.

What if I can't do less? I have bills to pay, a child to support, a future to protect. Responsibilities and a level of busyness that I cannot always just step away from. It rankles.

But now, in the midst of all this, there is a definite need for more me-time than might usually be required. A need to take myself off somewhere to recoup.

I decide to plan a break on my own, or at least one without my daughter.

Chapter 46

Upside-Down

For a long time, I had wanted to try an actual yoga retreat, but the prospect of holidaying with strangers, and the possible crustiness of said strangers, put me off.

So, I invented a homemade yoga retreat. No strangers, no crustiness. My father was going to their apartment in Spain for a two-week break, and I gate-crashed four days of his trip. Even planning the itinerary was a tonic.

I had come across Carla, a yoga teacher with a white cube of a studio clad in vivid pink bougainvillea near the apartment in Spain. Carla is an Icelandic yoga teacher. Imagine a sort of Helena Christensen in yoga gear, with the same suggestion of warrior in her physicality.

As it happens, Carla has been separated twice, so not only completely understands my situation, but provides a comforting blueprint of woman-who-is-flourishing-post-separation.

Carla doesn't believe in one long relationship for life. 'You talk only about the child, darling. All my exes adore me. I make it all about what is best for the children,' she tells me firmly. I begin to think maybe things could be OK.

Apart from the yoga, I plan to spend my days reading on the beach, if I feel like it, not speaking to anyone for hours – certainly not bringing anyone to the bathroom or working out what snack I will next provide.

Nothing else to think about. Heaven.

Dad picks me up at the airport and we immediately begin planning what we will eat for the four days. What day shall we have steak? Which night shall we eat out at our favourite beachside restaurant for salmon and chips? There's something incredibly peaceful about holidaying with my father. The undemanding, calm solidity of him. At night, we watch the second series of *Stranger Things*, both working on our laptops.

Carla teaches aerial yoga – yoga that takes place in a swing, much of it upside-down.

I have never been the kind of person who could do handstands or cartwheels. However, neither have I ever been the kind of person who thought their marriage would be over before one of us actually died. When that happens, you need to rethink what kind of person you are. Throw things upside-down. Make a small act of bravery in order to reassure yourself that you are capable of bigger ones.

I treat myself to a course of one-to-one classes, if only because I want all Carla's attention trained on me when I fling myself upside-down in this fabric swing.

'I'm very tired, I don't want to do any of the workout stuff, just the yoga bits,' I tell her at our first class. She ignores me entirely. We spend the first part of our session doing crunches and squats in mid-air. Afterwards, I am insufferable – is there anything as unbearably smug as a person who works out while away on holiday?

Aerial yoga allows for stretches that are not possible when you're anchored to the ground. You stretch out like a flat plank, and then find your limbs can go further, your arms and legs curl back behind your torso, until you are an upside-down crab. Floating in the air, nothing limits your movements. I can feel the tension of months peeling off. And it's nice to feel able to do something I never thought I would, even if it is only a very poor imitation of a handstand while held in a harness.

The first day I have the kind of headache that turns to nausea in your stomach, only bearable by sleeping it off. I know it is stress that has been deeply imbedded in my body, and which is now finding its way out.

It feels like a luxury to be able to address it. To not just guzzle down two Nurofen Plus and push through. To stop and do what I need to do. No pressing work, no child. No deadline to be met, no food to be prepared. 'If you can't solve what is going on in your mind, look at your body. How does if feel? Deal with that,' Helen the counsellor tells me.

Back in Dublin, I see a post on Instagram for a weekend aerial-yoga course, and Sophie and I book tickets. It's a sort of lighter, introductory version of what I'd done with Carla, a fact I waste no time in letting Sophie know, temporarily gaining the upper wellness hand.

It's in a room in one of those redbrick buildings in George's Street, an old studio on the first floor, all clouded mirrors, steepled windows and high ceilings. Colourful fabrics hang from the ceiling.

For most of it, we joke around, enjoy the newness, the time to ourselves, this short break from being a mother of small children and the hustle of being self-employed. And then the last move, swinging upside down. I charge our rope, jump up and flip myself upside down. And there it is again, that jolt of adrenaline. Delight in my own bravery.

Sometimes, you need to turn everything upside-down in order to find a way to fix it. To know that you can.

Chapter 47

The Witching Hour

I've never been a big fan of Hallowe'en, although I am grudgingly coming to enjoy it – having a daughter who lives to wear costumes and considers it a high point of her year helps.

Like her, our neighbourhood goes big on Hallowe'en. They make a week-long celebration of it. On the day itself, after the trick or treating, everyone gathers at the community centre where there is a selection of handmade banners, ghouls, ghosts and goblins, to choose from. There's a float blaring out music, a band and dancers, and we all walk behind it for about an hour, in and out through the winding streets of terraced houses, ending up at the central playground, in which a haunted house has been created in a large tent.

Two years ago, we were the *Frozen* family, Elsa (my daughter, of course), Anna (me) and her father Christoph. My brother and father were apparently Olaf and Sven, although with little evidence of costumes. She had been sick all week, was just feeling better and had rallied and insisted on the parade, sitting up on her father's shoulders, her chin resting on his head. We snuck off home as it passed our house. This year, we are witches. I don't think I normally fall into the trap of overcompensating because of what has happened, but, for some reason, Hallowe'en brings it out in me, a sort of urge for perfection.

I make the entire family dress up and come on the parade, even though it is raining. They all plod along grimly behind us – politely informing me that the following year they will definitely not be staying for the entire thing.

My daughter and I nearly come to blows before we leave the house. She has been planning her look for weeks – a green face to go with the witch's costume. But when I finally go to scrabble about in the box amongst the crayons, there is face paint in every colour but green.

'I have just the thing,' I announce on the verge of hysteria, trying to ward off her own incipient meltdown. I pull an unused eyeshadow palette from my drawer, in which there is a dark green. 'It's awfullllll,' my daughter cries when she looks at my handiwork in the mirror, her face daubed in streaks of green shimmer.

Chapter 48

How to Declutter

'What you need to do is get Sarah Reynolds in here,' Sophie gasped as she and her boys spilled into our living room, having squeezed past the scooters, several to-go-to-the-charity-shop bags, and various other things cluttering up our small hall, and turning it into a sort of obstacle course.

'Apparently all her clients have either suffered a death or divorce,' she says triumphantly, in the manner of one who has just produced a rabbit from a hat.

This turns out to be not exactly true, Sarah herself tells me when she arrives. Sarah is a professional organiser, and I am interviewing her for a piece. She's so convincing I then hire her to do a session in my house. 'It's not too bad,' she reassures me. 'I've seen much worse.'

Her manner is a mixture of your favourite teacher at school – the one who never had to raise their voice to keep control, who even when they got cross always had something of a glint in their eye – and Mary Poppins. No nonsense. 'Ah, ah, ah,' she says, shaking her head at the sight of me trotting off to the kitchen with some clutter.

That is not the method. The method is one room at a time, which is very on brand for me at this time; when everything is about one day at a time. We spend three hours in my living room, and they rank as amongst the most enjoyable hours of that first year. The sense of ignoring the outside world and the to-do list and focusing entirely on making my living space feel calmer.

Somehow, and without me telling her, Sarah clocks that paperwork is where the problem really lies. Life administration I put in a pile and then put off. There is always a pressing deadline to work to, a more immediate fire to be put out – and then, exhausted, I put off the pile of letters and bills and things to be chased or dealt with.

Procrastination. Quite common, I'm told, in times of grief.

'I think I'm going to take three days off and blitz through it,' I tell Helen when we discuss how much life-admin procrastination is stressing me out. 'I heard it,' I continue, when she raises a quizzical eyebrow; we both know I am being ridiculous, this will not happen.

'Just try and do half an hour each day,' she suggests.

'Make a list of three things each day,' Judith adds when I tell her. 'They can be even very tiny things. You will build momentum.'

Sarah's good at this stuff, at looking at the innards of your house, your life, and seeing the places where you are not on top of things, but not making you feel judged. She too has had a big break-up, she tells me, and understands this grief of the life you had planned vanishing.

In a pile of paperwork, we come across my marriage certificate. She holds it up, 'For filing?' And we burst out laughing, insiders in the grief of a lost relationship.

Watching her walk about the house muttering to herself about where things could go in the manner of someone playing Tetris with my belongings is very soothing, I trail happily in the wake of her effortless capability, soothed by the fact of someone else being temporarily in charge.

In my bedroom, she suggests that I leave some space in the closet I have taken over in the aftermath of my husband's departure, for the possibility of a future new occupant. 'Good feng shui.'

I chortle at her. 'Nobody else is getting into this house,' I say. This is my daughter's house.

Chapter 49

The Woo-Woo Club

'You've clearly become a fully signed-up member of the woo-woo club,' my friend Julia says. It's a cold winter night. My daughter's upstairs asleep, I'm sitting on my couch working. In France, Julia is doing the same thing. We were having a WhatsApp conversation about anxiety – hers is an almost lifelong burden she has shouldered; mine is more of a due-to-current-circumstances visitor.

When I first began working as a journalist, Julia, already well established, took me under her wing, guided me and saved me missteps. We worked all week together, then went out every Friday night, ending up in her flat, or my house with Rachel, sharing a bed, lounging for hours in the morning chatting and nursing our hangovers. She moved to London and I missed her dreadfully. Shortly after she left, I met my husband, and he became the person I lounged around with at the weekend.

Now, she has been listening to me extolling on the virtues of crystals.

It was the third time that week that a friend had mentioned the phrase to me. 'The universe is clearly giving me a sign', is exactly the kind of statement that I would have snorted in derision at during my pre-woo-woo club membership days, but which I now say to myself. When you are non-religious, you can feel a little allergic to anything that seems a bit, well, made up. A bit fantastical. It is simply not your way. If only because you get a bit generally allergic to people unable to accept that you might feel more than enough with what you have. That being non-religious is not to feel a lack.

Also, when your life has been relatively smooth and easy, you do not need to go looking for things.

'When you are cracked open, you become open,' Michael the meditator said.

'I'm definitely coming around to the value of a bit of woo-woo for the soul as life goes on,' Julia, also a person who would previously have laughed up her sleeve at such things, continues.

I go out for dinner with Ruth, my original first wife. We meet every couple of months, ostensibly for a catch-up, in reality much of it involves me running through a checklist, to which she kindly replies to each point, 'Normal, same, me too.'

'Ah,' she says, when I mention my goings on. 'You've joined the woo-woo club.'

The woo-woo club isn't actually as for the birds as that title might imply. In fact, it isn't for the birds at all.

It is the yoga and the reiki, the crystals and the chanting, the choir groups, retreats, knitting clubs and crafts groups that are building up around us. Clusters of women, getting together to do some sort of activity the main purpose of which is to allow them to take a step back from life, create a moment out, and to bring their stress levels down.

That is its main purpose.

There's also the lovely side effect of tapping into a network of women. I know it can be hard to make new friends as an adult, especially after a separation, when you feel raw, and vulnerable, and as if everyone else is tucked away in safe, cosy domesticity. The book clubs, the music groups, the live podcast recording, talks, mums' gatherings; these are a way in.

Who wants to meet in a pub these days? None of my friends anyhow. This is how we socialise. And, for me, without another adult at home, I have to look outside for my support network.

I don't think it takes something as dramatic as a marriage falling apart for someone's stress levels to need to be taken down a few notches. Most of my friends are stressed in some aspect of their lives – they're all in the trenches with small kids and full-on jobs, wondering if they will ever get a mortgage, looking after parents who are unwell, struggling under a gruelling workload. Your thirties and forties are the time for that.

Every woman needs a woo-woo club. A further branch of your tribe. A group of women who will tell you it's OK, that they felt like that too, it's not just you. A subtle mesh that weaves around the fabric of your life, sustaining and supporting you. That creates a life pause, in which to take down the stress levels.

Chapter 50

Cracking up at *The Nutcracker*

'I hate this time of year,' a friend, also seperated, says to me. 'It's such a difficult time to be a single parent.' We're sitting watching our children play, it's the end of term and everyone is exhausted.

I know what she means, of course. The everyone-having-the-time-of-their-liveness of it. The expense. The scheduling. The complete fetishising of the 2.4 nuclear family.

But, at the same time I think, *No. Not me*. Nothing can diminish my love of Christmas. I do not understand people who complain about Christmas starting earlier each year. I would happily have Christmas from the first of September if I could. Several Christmases in to being separated, I would say I wax and wane with that. Some years are better than others. But that first Christmas, I almost felt a defiant determination that this would be enjoyable.

In honour of the fact that the Christmas season was upon us, we had decided to go big on our weekend town outing. Mo and Grandad had invited us to *The Nutcracker* ballet. Mo is a music teacher and has been telling my daughter the story since she was a baby.

We talk about it for weeks. What we will eat (Milano's margherita pizza, rainbow ice-cream) what treats we (she) will have, what ballet-inspired outfits we (she, hopefully) shall wear. We finally settle on shorts over leggings, her pineapple T-shirt and fairy wings, which are discarded five minutes after we leave the house, to be carried for the rest of the day by me.

She picks out a dress for me made in a sheer fabric with frills as my most ballet-ish look. 'This Mommy,' I am instructed.

I sometimes wonder if people imagine, given some of my work is in fashion and given my daughter's intense interest in clothes, that I am at home helicopter-schooling her in its ins and outs. 'No, it's Dolce *ampersand* Gabbana.' For the record, I am not. As soon as she turned two-and-a-half she began dictating exactly what she would wear.

We scooted through the park to get the DART, to meet my parents in town. It was one of those lovely slightly misty winter mornings. Halfway there, we stop, as we have planned, for a mini picnic; oranges on the bench in the middle of the park.

At the station, a train is due, and we run, herself ahead screaming, 'Come on, Mommy', me following, all scooter, fairy wings, tulle dress. My daughter leaps over the gap into the carriage, and suddenly begins screaming. 'My eyyyyyyyyyye. There's a rock in my eyyyyyyyyyyyyyyyyyyyyyyyye!'

This escalates quickly to 'I can't seeeeeeeeeee.'

'Try blinking,' I urge her, sympathy laced with suspicion. A child's ratio of scream-to-injury can be out of whack, so I'm not sure how bad this really is. Even something tiny in your eye can feel shockingly painful.

By the time we reach our station, things have escalated further. My daughter is wailing. She can't walk either, it would seem, so I carry her, the scooter, our backpack *and* the damn fairy wings.

We're both wearing our winter coats, shiny puffas, so she keeps slithering down my body; it's like trying to carry a weighted, slippy sleeping bag.

In my desperation, I have fixated on the idea that the only thing to do is make it to a particularly fancy optician two streets away. We make it down to the street in front of the station, where I try to hail a taxi, but none of them stop. There is no way I can carry both of us and our luggage all the way. Just then, a Garda car pulls up in front of us. A guard gets out and starts to fiddle with a barrier and a traffic cone by the side of the road.

Fuck it, I think. If I'm going to be a single mother to a child who tragically lost her sight on what should have been an idyllic family day out, then I'm getting full value for my taxes.

'Guard,' I bleat as pitifully as I can. 'She's losing her sight. Please, help us.'

He turns to take us in. My daughter has chosen this moment to stop crying and gnaw instead at the biscuit the size of her head I have pulled from our bag, worrying at a deeply embedded Skittle with her teeth. I'd imagine by now we look slightly feral.

'Get in,' he says in the voice of a man whose patience has been severely tried.

His kindness undid me, I suspect. This can be the only reason why, in the silence as we pull off, I choose to say to the two guards in the front, 'Anyone watch the Maurice McCabe documentary last night?'

They humour me, both smiling. 'Yes. We all did.'

To which I choose to reply 'Five kids. Amazing.' An awkward silence settles, herself munches away, crumbs spreading all over the back seat.

As we're about to get out, they turn the siren on for her and I want to hug them, but I've done enough here, so, thankfully, I resist.

We make it to the optician, where they try to conceal their horror at the sight of us, sweaty, sticky, shedding crumbs. We're ushered quickly downstairs and my daughter refuses to allow the optician to pour orange dye in her eye.

'She seems OK now anyway,' I suggest, broken enough that I am willing to take my chances.

'This is the worst day ever,' my daughter grumps afterwards as we walk up the street in the blinding sun. She's still working on the cookie.

I give her a look, raise an eyebrow. 'Going to enjoy this pizza and ice-cream now, are you?' I say. We burst out laughing.

It becomes a joke between us, when we're having a particularly good time. 'This is the worst day *ever*,' she will say, a wicked glint in her eye.

Chapter 51

Life Audit

Things swing from intense stress to a feeling of I *can do this.*

'It's the pendulum,' Judith tells me, describing the extremes you must endure after the difficult parts of life. 'Things will swing back and forth until life settles again,' she explains. 'It won't always feel like this.'

Sometimes, I imagine I am pulling myself out of a swamp of difficulty. At the times when things feel particularly bad, like I am trapped in some kind of compressor and it is squeezing me for all it's worth, I tell myself that this is because I am pulling an entire limb out of the swamp. Hard now, but it will make it easier afterwards

'It's not because you're going backwards, it's because

you're going forwards,' Shereen tells me one day on the phone.

The Christmas hysteria has been all a bit much. I'm having a week where it feels like I could quite easily disappear into a cave, so I make myself ring her and Sophie each day. If they haven't heard from me, they check in.

When I tell Judith about the swamp (there's also one where I am holding a massive boulder between my shoulders, and I'm slowly trying to stand up and shake it off), she looks delighted.

'Use that,' she says instantly. 'What happens next? You're out of the swamp, you decide now.'

I imagine myself washing all the muck off.

It is my birthday. Until now, getting older had never bothered me. Waging a war against an inevitability such as the physical aspects of ageing seems too pointless a battle to even contemplate engaging with. And also, I would rather not be on the side that presumes the signs of ageing to be a bad thing.

At other birthdays, I had always had everything I wanted. Career. House. Husband, Child. One by one, they had all fallen into place. Separation, though, engenders an unwanted, unasked-for life audit. A putting your life on the weighing scales and seeing how it measures up.

'Imagine I didn't have her,' I say to Lewine one day when we sit in the courtyard at the park, watching our children scoot after each other – my daughter and her son battling it out over whether they will play ponies or football. I would make another life for myself if I didn't have her, I know that.

But I do have her, and having her helps me to feel like I can manage all of this. I have had to imagine, and then create, my life without the person I thought I would spend it with. Now, in the back-and-forth invisible negotiations I make in my head of what I need to be happy, the whittling down to what it will take, I find that I can hand back a husband because I get to keep a child. She is my non-negotiable.

Chapter 52

An A-Z of How to Co-parent

'I just think it's so saaaaaaaaad when I see families who don't speak or where the parents don't spend time with each other together with the kids,' a friend said to me in doleful tones, while also patting my hand approvingly.

'I think it's just so wonderful the way you guys have managed to do things. I always think it's *such* a shame when people cannot work things out amicably, for the sake of the children. That they have somehow let everyone down. Let their *children* ... down,' she continues, with extra pause for effect.

The third friend in our party winces, and I see her bridle. I can tell she, too, disagrees. She's a psychologist, so she knows about these things. *Really* knows. That mostly, everyone is probably doing their best within a situation of pressure-cooker levels of stress. And that, in a divorce, you are not necessarily operating with a full buffet of choices.

It is just days after Christmas and we're at another gathering, sitting squashed around a table facing into a further round of turkey and stuffing. She means well, this friend who is delivering her views on co-parenting, by way of a review of how we have just spent Christmas (together, all at my parents' house) but I want to shout at her, *Just stay in your lane.*

It's great, that we did this. But it is not really down to anything we have done better than others who are co-parenting. We don't have superior co-parenting skills and our will to make this as right as it can be for our child is not stronger than that of people who do not manage to get to a place of amicability where they can contemplate spending Christmas together, without risking the day turning into a battleground.

'We were just lucky,' I want to say. 'Who knows what we'll do next year?'

I want to tell her that in co-parenting, most people are not actively choosing to not do well by their children. That most of us want the best, but that, sometimes, it simply does not work out like that, and you have to do the best given the circumstances you are in. What that best looks like, who's to say?

Instead, I grip the stem of my wine glass tightly.

'We're just lucky,' I say again through gritted teeth. 'It's more luck really, than anything we did.'

Because, let's be honest, in the minefield of co-parenting, strewn with everything from the corpses of best intentions, to unexploded bombs of rage, how you intend things to go is usually quite far from how they do go.

You may set out thinking, *We'll go on annual holidays together. This will be wonderful,* and then find that what really works is for you to see as little as possible of each other. Or somewhere in between those two extremes.

Even Gwyneth, the high priestess of doing these things consciously, has admitted that she may, in fact, have been somewhat off the mark.

That thing married people say, about how they never got divorced, merely because neither of them wanted a divorce at the same time? For divorced people who are co-parenting, it probably goes something like, *We never killed each other because both of us were never murderous at quite the same moment.*

Nobody gets through a divorce or a separation, where you need to find a new way to behave towards each other because there are children involved, without crashing up against each other repeatedly and painfully, before things hopefully settle.

Married people don't have the same boundaries as other relationships, which is fine in a loving relationship that works, but disastrous when things end. You need to detach from the person but then create an entire new relationship with them because you're parents.

You will need to rebuild boundaries appropriate for the new relationship you are attempting to create. This will take time, don't worry about that. You will probably behave a certain way a number of times before you realise that that way no longer works and you need to set a boundary.

And setting boundaries feels really uncomfortable, partly because you are saying no where you are used to saying yes. That feeling of discomfort does go away, it does get easier.

This chapter started out with the intention of being an actual A–Z on co-parenting, a guide, inasmuch as anyone can give a guide to such a thing. And then I thought, *Who the hell am I to advise anyone in such a definitive manner?* In reality, we're all making it up as we go along. Co-parenting is like when children are very young; things work for a couple of months, and then need to be changed. If only because your child and their needs keep changing, so you also adjust around them.

We are all doing our best for our children, given our own stress levels.

Whatever your best looks like – family holidays together or handovers through a third party because you simply cannot bear to be in the same room as each other – inside the bubble, we all know most of us are trying our best. That best may simply look a little off-centre to the outside world.

They can jog on.

What advice I do have, is below.

Anger is going to happen between you. I used to think that it would dissipate once the decision to split was made. No longer trying and failing to make the relationship work, we would stop bumping heads and go back to the easy friendship we once enjoyed. It took me ages (much longer than this rather obvious fact should have taken) to realise that the anger wouldn't simply disappear.

In fact, I didn't realise this – Helen the counsellor told me, most likely frustrated at watching me fail to understand this very basic reality.

'Just because you have ended the marriage, you are still the same people,' she patiently explained. 'The same things will most likely still bother you about each other.' So, find a way to deal with the anger within the relationship.

There is big anger – things you still haven't forgiven each other for – and small anger – day-to day-irritants, passive-aggressive comments or just the way they do things.

If the relationship is definitely over, then big anger is probably best dealt with in counselling. Your conversation is no longer with your spouse, but with yourself and a professional, who will help you forgive, accept and move on. That is what will serve you best, not arguing past happenings into the ground until you are both exhausted, and further away than ever from figuring out some way to exist together as the parents you still are and always will be.

For small anger, pick your battles. Some things are worth speaking up about; for others it's best to let them slide. Decide on your non-negotiables and focus on getting those in a line.

My very wise friend Kate Gunn, wrote in *Untying the Knot* that in most of her and her ex-husband's big discussions, neither one of them came away feeling delighted with the result. Because they were compromising. You can choose to battle to the very edge of your sanity on something or you can choose an outcome you can both live with.

You will have expectations. It's probably best to let them go – or at the very least, manage them. How you think co-parenting will look when you first split will quite likely be very different from how it ends up looking. You may never take those family holidays you first thought possible, and you will get to a point where you are OK with that.

Chapter 53

The Retreat

Christmas was over and January had never felt so daunting. It is now half a year since we had separated. My friend Karen is running a retreat for Nollaig na mBan, and Sophie and I go to cover it for the paper, both of us by now in possession of a fully blown wellness hobby that is fast becoming an expensive habit to feed.

The retreat has been designed to celebrate the power of female energy. 'What we're all about nowadays,' Soph and I congratulate each other smugly in the car, speeding down the motorway away from our responsibilities.

Yoga instructor Lou Horgan is leading events. It was my first time meeting Lou – I had never heard of her, but she enjoys something of a cult following in the world of yoga. There is something leonine about her; all tawny skin and blonde hair. I instantly imprint on her and begin a silent best-girl-in-class-one-upmanship with Soph, who, having attended Lou's pregnancy classes, has an edge.

The retreat is arranged around yoga classes and eating. 'Nothing restrictive on the menu,' Lou assures us, dismissing the idea of the sort of miserable-punish-yourself food January sees so much of.

Lou begins with a talk, setting out her stall, so to speak. 'Yoga,' she explains, 'was invented by men, for men. It is in fact the oldest boys' club in the world. Many of the traditional moves were not created with women's bodies in mind, so women's needs are not always met through traditional yoga teachings.'

It's like most of the world, designed with men in mind. 'It's that thing we're all realising now, that all of the maps of how we live are trialled on men,' Lou says to me later. 'All of the structures have been projected from a male vantage point, and we're so adaptable as women and we're so capable, that we just kind of mush our way into the shape or the form that was created. Because to put your hand up and say, 'Well, it's different for me. How does that work for me?' would draw attention to the fact that, maybe, you're just not as good as a man. We're always trying to fit into the mould. But the very best we can be in that mould is not a man.'

Lou has been practising yoga for over twenty years. Her philosophy is to align yourself with the rhythms and cycles of the natural world. 'Men's and women's energy cycles are different,' she explains. 'A man's is daily, twenty-four hours; a women's is monthly.'

It's the first time I've ever heard anyone point this out. To urge a room full of women to respect the different energy levels they experience throughout the month rather than constantly forcing themselves to push through.

To hibernate when we need to.

'There is an in-built rest period built into your body,' she says of women's monthly cycles. 'And it's not taken, and then women get to menopause and they are wrecked. The number-one symptom that I see in most women is exhaustion, and an attitude of 'How can I get over this without having to feel anything?"

It seems like the most sensible thing I'd heard in a long time, particularly in the face of the post-Christmas fear simmering within me. Ideally you wouldn't need it, could decide upon it of your own accord, but Lou provides a sort of permission to actually examine and respond to my own needs and current capabilities.

One of the reasons I had hesitated at the idea of a group retreat was the thought of all that time with strangers. I examine that thought now and realise how much has changed. I relish the dinner.

'It's so beautiful, when women get to be around just

women,' Lou says. 'It's our nature to carry. We carry the baby, we carry the water, we carry the emotional needs of others. Wouldn't it be amazing, to once a month down tools, and be with each other, support each other in our shared experience?'

Being with this group of women turns out to be one of the nicest parts of the retreat.

'It's a shame it's not a week with these people,' Sophie says after dinner as we walk back through the kitchen garden across the bridge and alongside the pond to our room. We ring front desk but the rooms are booked out for the next night, so we must return home.

Chapter 54
The Talismans

'I'll tell you a secret,' someone says to me. They are slightly tipsy, a little leery. I was on a night out with some work people, it's come to the messy end of the evening and I was just about to leave. I can see they are delighted with whatever unpleasantness they are about to impart on me – and also that I am unlikely to enjoy it. 'That dent on your finger? It never really goes away.' We both look at the fourth finger on my left hand.

My wedding ring wasn't a traditional wedding ring, and so, for a time, I thought I might get away with wearing it again eventually. Repurpose it, put it on another finger. I'm not so sure now that it will ever be sufficiently divested of its original meaning for me to put it on and not feel a jolt of some sort every time I look at it.

I had chosen it and the engagement ring weeks before we got engaged, and taken to visiting the shop on occasion to try them on, whenever I was in town for work. One day, passing by, I stopped to go in again, and then thought no, this is getting embarrassing. If I had, I would have found the engagement ring gone. He proposed the next day. There is a photo in my phone of us afterwards coming down from the mountain where we had gone for a walk I had reluctantly agreed too, our faces both shiny with happiness. On our way to tell my parents. I hate to look at it, but cannot bear to delete it.

The engagement ring had a tiny turtle symbol on it. Slow, but always wins the race, always gets there; we had decided it was a symbol, as if it was within our purview to award ourselves such certainty. Choosing symbols, it turns out, won't protect you.

A year before we separated, I'd lost my wedding ring. I remember taking it off and putting it in my locker at the gym, and then forgetting to take it out afterwards. I reordered, a size larger now, because shredding for the wedding doesn't last, and thought no more about it.

The night my husband moved out, as he was organising his things in the car, he found it – the original wedding ring. Hidden between the back seat and the door. So now I have two. I'll give them to my daughter someday. Or make earrings out of them.

My wedding veil sits in the dressing-up box amongst her Elsa, Spanish Princess and Skye Paw Patrol costumes, just one more layer of tulle in with the Disney Princess costumes. She went through a phase of playing weddings, which was my fault. The morning after a slumber party at my parents, she and Mo and I spent a few hours in our pyjamas watching Meghan and Harry's wedding.

'Would you look at her mother?' I kept saying, hoping she would soak up the sight of this wonderfully dignified single mother, on her own but just fine, and so proud of her girl. Doria was the reason I had wanted her to watch this in the first place. 'Isn't she fabulous?'

I should have known, her four-year-old princess-obsessed eyes were trained firmly on Meghan and her dress and veil.

'We're playing weddings,' she announces when her little friend Jayden from next door comes for a playdate.

I imagine I will push the dress on her when she attends college balls (this is not quite as obnoxiously helicoptering as it sounds, it is an evening dress, not a wedding dress). One day when she was two-and-a-half, I had allowed her to try it on in dress-up. With the Jimmy Choos to match, she tottered back and forth between me and her grandmother in her bedroom. The low back meant her edible baby bum poked out, like that soap star who once thought going on the red-carpet with a bum-cleavage-revealing dress was a good idea.

I miss my engagement ring the most. The small turtle shape in opal on a rose-gold band, a symbol of our imagined solidity.

Gradually though, the pieces get replaced. The mums-group girls give me a necklace from my favourite shop for my birthday. My daughter gives me a beaded one on the same occasion, having spent two hours, her father tells me, choosing the beads in the shop. 'It's on green thread, Mommy,' she points out, 'your favourite colour.' Shereen gives me a bangle. There is Merle's 'today' necklace.

In Marbella later in the year, I decide it is time to try rings again, and buy myself a huge green one, as different as I can find from the delicate marital rings.

The dent on my finger is still there. Only I can see its faint outlines now, just at the side of my finger where it meets the next one. It may never fully disappear. It is the dent of a big loss after all. It doesn't go away, it simply gets easier to bear. Or the rest of your life gets bigger around it, dwarfing it, and its place in your life becomes smaller.

I can live with the dent.

Chapter 55

Are You on Tinder?

I was twenty-six when I met my ex-husband. When the marriage ends, I am nearly forty.

Now, I need to figure out all the layers of my new self. Who am I without him, a person who has propped me up in places where I am weak, as I have done for him. A couple grow together like one organism.

Much of marriage is passing back and forth between you the duty of being the currently calm person and the currently freaking-out one. If I woke in the middle of the night, worried about all the things that needed doing, we would make a list together and that took away the anxiety.

I hear him gently calming down our daughter now in the same voice.

Who am I without a husband? Who am I when I am not a wife? I need to round out those parts of me that were propped up by him.

I write a feature on what it is like to be single over the age of thirty-five. Several of the women I interview tell me that, after their own break-up, they were cut from dinner-party circuits they knew were still in existence. They thought it was partly because they were now viewed as a threat to domestic harmony, partly an embarrassment. Would they destabilise the marriages of others? Would they be too upset at the sight of a table of couples? Throw off the perfect balance of a divisible number of guests?

They were invited to lunches or occasional midweek kitchen suppers. But weekend dinner parties? Never.

Not for the first time, I am grateful for my own circles of friends who would deem the presence of menfolk a hindrance to a get-together, in the way of a proper catch-up. Surplus. School girls, mum friends, work friends, book clubs – all circles that happen to exclude men, so no one needs to worry that I might collapse at the sight of one.

Who am I without being a wife and the future that that implied, the family life that will now not come to be? In the last days of deciding that our marriage was over, I was hit by a whole new wave of grief as I realised we would not retire together. That the man I had watched so lovingly tend to his mother as she lay dying in hospital, of whom I had thought, as I looked on at such care, *I'm so glad I will get old with him*, would in fact be in my old age something of a stranger. That my daughter would by then know him far more than me. Unfathomable.

At the time, the thought, one I hadn't previously considered, was almost enough to rethink the separation. 'That's future thinking,' I know Helen would tell me, cautioning against projecting too far into the future, of worrying about things I cannot control, that might not even happen, and overwhelming myself by doing so.

'Somehow I don't think you will be retiring alone,' friends say with a smile when I mention this to them. And I know they mean it kindly and reassuringly, but I don't see it. It took until I was twenty-six to find my person.

And anyway, this is a post-man situation. I do not want to fix it by finding a new man. I do not want to think that the *only* way to fix it lies in finding another man.

My daughter is right, this is our home. There is no space for a third.

Chapter 56

Things You Should Know About Sadness and Grief

Sometimes the second year is harder. You're bracing yourself in the first, for all those firsts. And everyone around you is so aware. In the second, people forget. And you relax a little, so are taken unawares when it hits. As you get a bit stronger, it's like grief knows you're are more able for it. You can take in what has happened, as the shock recedes.

Writing articles about grief being over is a sure-fire way of ensuring the next *day* will be a grief day. You are not done with grief until it has decided it is done with you.

You cannot outrun, out-yoga, out-meditate or out-sleep grief. These things can help you from going under entirely, and may encourage the mist to clear a little faster, but they will not vanquish it. Grief demands its time and place.

It is possible to be very happy generally, and still have days where you are felled by the grief. Slowly it will shift. You will realise you are not sad about your daily life, and that you no longer become sad daily. Now you're sad about the past or the future. But at least not the present.

Sadness is different from grief. Grief needs to be got through: ignore it at your peril. Sadness needs to be accommodated. You may never be fully purged of it, but you will learn to live with it.

Chapter 57

The Big Day

I am getting ready to go to my first wedding since we separated. I am going on my own, meeting friends when I get there, all old (in length of the friendship, not age), all in couples.

This should feel sad or daunting, but, right now in my bedroom, I'm just enjoying the freedom of getting ready to go out without the company of a small child determined to 'help' and be involved.

After she broke into a Tom Ford eye palette, a gift I was hiding in a drawer, and used the smoky colour to draw black X marks across each shade, I bought my daughter her own, a cheap palette from the chemist, all greens and purples. I think it's meant to be for concealing tired adult eyes, but the colours work well with the *Frozen* sisters' palette. So now, when I put on make-up, she face paints.

She's having a slumber party with her grandparents and, in her absence, I'm actually curling my hair, rather than just giving it quick blast dry at the front and hoping the back can look after itself.

I try on a few options before deciding on one, rather than grabbing the first thing from my wardrobe. As always on a day that might prove challenging, I like to have something of my gran's about me, on this occasion her navy velvet dress coat. I remember that the last time I wore it was at our civil ceremony and quickly dismiss the thought. Caught up in organising the big event, we had forgotten to book the civil one, and so it took place two months afterwards, followed by a party at my parents' house. After the solemnity and the big crowd of the main event, this one was laced with a sort of relieved hysteria; off their best behaviour, grateful for the lack of formality, everyone was giddy and quick to laugh throughout the ceremony. Back at my parents' house, surrounded by his family and mine, by children I had known since they were babies, who now I see only on social media, I had thought *this is our life, and this is one of many such gatherings.*

It's often not the things you think you will feel sad about that are the ones that actually make you sad. It's often not the big things, the out-of-the-ordinary, once-in-a-lifetime events – they are not what really make up the fabric of a life. It's the small paper cuts that really hurt. The minutiae, much of which was unseen by anyone but the two of you. You'll never share your favourite meal again. The thing they cooked better than anyone else, you will never eat that again. Steak is one of my favourite meals, and no one cooked it better than him, and now I just can't.

I didn't feel sad to be going to a wedding when my own marriage has fallen apart, something that surprises me – but, then, I don't feel sad about my own wedding. I wore a dress that cost €130 (I'm still smug at not having succumbed to a ball of ivory silk that cost thousands only to sit in my wardrobe). For one day and night, all our friends and family ate and partied in one place. My great aunt, my sister-in-law, my uncle, people who are no longer here now.

The sadness comes out in other, unexpected ways. I have a friend, a work acquaintance, who got married in the same venue just before us. We planned together. Ever since the split, I have avoided her; the sight of the different route her life has taken – still married, two kids – is too much. I feel bad about it, as if I'm unfairly taking things out on her, but I just can't face her.

Often it is the smaller things, the things that seep in through the cracks, that make you sad. In between relishing the peace and quiet in which I was putting on my make-up, I *was* a bit sad, it's there, below me, a trough into which I could always fall at any moment. I would miss my husband as my partner-in-crime at this wedding.

The person you marry is the person with whom you filter the world through. Process it with. He was the most fun person to attend a wedding with. To get through the marathon slog that such days can be. We would go in as a unit, ready to enjoy, to secretly mock a little, to let loose and to know when it was time to leave.

Just before we separated, I went to a wedding on my own. Before I left there was a row. In the church the priest was ridiculous, a self-appointed comedian. And I cried discreetly to myself at how much my husband would have enjoyed it, how we would have leaned in to each other, trying not to laugh. And I cried at the thought of how far from that we were.

In planning our own wedding, he had suggested early on that we view every decision through the filter of 'Will this improve the party we are throwing for our guests?' It seemed like a good objective with which to plan the day. I think it is why, now, I can look back on it and not feel sad. A party with everyone you love and many you like. Still not sad, despite everything.

It set us on a road to our daughter and divorce hasn't changed that.

I walk into this wedding on my own, which isn't as nerve-wracking as I might have thought. I have future-proofed for this moment, meeting this gang at a birthday party the week before. That had been an ordeal, though, walking in to their slightly frozen smiles; I had put off seeing them for months. I had also made my brother and Song Yue come with me, and we had a great night. It seems funny now, that there was a time when I did not feel able for seeing people at all, even people I had known all my life.

The ways you think you will feel forever, you won't. You will forget you even felt that way in the first place. That a thing was difficult, or sad. That you struggled with it.

It is strange to be a party of one. To have no insider with whom to critique the hor d'oeuvres, the speeches, the meal, the band. A person to turn to in the lulls between small talk. There's no one to easily fall back on. Instead, I have to be alert for those moments, be ready to casually move to another group. To be the one to decide, on my own, that it is time to quietly nip out. We had always been good at that, deciding to leave at the same time. Suddenly tiring of it, finding each other across a room. But it is fun too, as if I am somehow under the radar. I can do exactly as I please.

I find support in unexpected places. Before the ceremony, I am braced, holding myself in against the fear that I might start crying uncontrollably when the music begins. An old friend's father sits beside me, a man I have known all my life, a man known for his kindness. He lost his own wife to illness not so long ago. He knows that I am separated.

'So, you've been through a rough time,' he says quietly, as we chat in whispers, heads bowed together, as those around us shout greetings at each other. For a moment I think his kindness might undo me. I have avoided his son for months for much the same reason, he has the same kindness that could crack you open.

But then the strings begin to play, he bows his head and his shoulders fold inwards, and I can feel the raw sadness rolling off him in waves. It's all I can do not to put my arms around him. I forget my own sadness entirely.

At the meal, a woman I don't know offers up her own story of separation, that of her parents. I know she is saying kindly, *... and look at me now, I am fine.*

I decide to leave just before the dancing starts, quietly proud of myself for surviving, for enjoying what felt like a particularly exposing event. My first wedding after my own marriage has fallen apart. I have pushed the bruise, and found it less tender than I would have thought.

But hitting the dance floor without my husband feels like a step too far. Unnecessary, to prove to myself that I can do it. I'm not sure if I can, anyway. Expose myself to that moment where everyone else has turned towards their other half. Or, worse, feel the kindness of friends, including me in their circle.

I say a quick goodbye, grab my coat and quietly sneak off. Outside it is freezing, and my feet in heels hurt but I decide to walk for a while. The streets are full of the Saturday-night crowd, and I slip between them, wrapped in my grandmother's velvet, running home to my daughter.

My mother is still up when I get home. 'How did it go?' she asks, half-looking for the gossip of the day, half-anxious for me.

'It was lovely,' I say. 'A great day.'

Chapter 58

Timetabling

'Want me to come over tonight?' my mother says down the phone. It's Wednesday, her night. After my daughter's father moved out, I had set about instigating a schedule. Creating it felt like the study schedules I made during my Leaving Cert year, the satisfaction of filling in all those little boxes of time, parsing out each hour, as if by this allotting of a task to each unit of time I could control the low-lying sense of panic that the year of big exams brought. Comfort in control – or, at least, the illusion of control. Having the ability to create it, the support of four other adults just across the way, makes me feel at times like calling myself a single parent is fraudulent, such support do I have.

Mondays my brother and his girlfriend, Song Yue,

come over in the evening to do dinner, bath and bedtime. The idea is that I go to yoga but, more often than not, I just sit on the couch catching up on work and enjoying the sight of two other adults in the house taking over. Of watching the chores happening, my daughter being put to bed, but not having to be the one to do them.

Tuesdays Grandad comes for dinner, chicken roast. Wednesdays my mother is available for slumber parties if needed (when she does stay, I insist we watch *Law & Order*, something I cannot do now that there is not another adult in the house, too scared turning off lights and going to bed alone afterwards).

And so on. Family either there or on call if needed.

But now, something feels different. Like I might no longer need the stabilisers of such regimented help. I can do it on my own. More, I want to. To kick off the crutches. I want it to be just the two of us. This is our reality now and I want to stop pretending otherwise. It's not that everything suddenly feels absolutely better. But I want to experiment with the loneliness and the sadness when they arrive. Do nothing to chase them away. To see if I am able for them.

I drop the schedule. We're ready to free style.

'No, it's grand thanks. We're going to have an early night,' I tell my mother.

Chapter 59

How to Dress for When Things Fall Apart

I had been waiting until my daughter was asleep in bed to open the parcel that had arrived late that dark January afternoon. When she finally dropped off, I came downstairs again and retrieved it from the hall, where it is hidden behind the table.

I place it on the couch and go to make a cup of tea. There it sat, large, satisfyingly squashy, the black-and-white print of an ASOS parcel. I slit it open with the scissors, and the contents spill out on to my wooden floor, a bundle of five colourful dresses, some floral, some as if they have been spattered in paint. It is the depths of winter, those mid-month weeks when Christmas, and next pay day, both feel years away. But I had treated myself and bought five dress reduced in the final days of the sales.

Shortly after my husband had moved out, I went to Marks & Spencer and bought the longest, most voluminously enveloping dressing gown I could find. Floor length, dark purple, with a roomy hood; it had felt positively *Star Wars*-ish.

Going to bed, I would carefully cover all corners of myself with the dressing gown, before putting the duvet over both of us, my dressing gown and I. A sort of protective layer of fleecy softness between me and the world.

Clothes became merely functional, their point simply what could they could offer me in the way of practical comfort, rather than as things of pleasure.

Much of my work is around fashion: formerly a buyer, I'm now a journalist. I have a ridiculously large wardrobe. But for months, as our marriage crumbled, I would stand in front of it and just feel a sense of overwhelm at the prospect of putting together an outfit.

To get through, you need to boil things down to the essentials. There are things you must do. Jettison everything else. Whenever I could get away with it, I wore black gym gear.

Getting through a crisis requires all your energy. And when all your energy is devoted to simply getting through the day, then stuff you enjoyed previously can become an onerous task. Something you have to do, rather than want to. Even seeing your best friends can feel like a chore.

Dressing up and putting on make-up are really ways of looking after yourself. Tending to yourself, because you are a thing worth taking care of. 'I'm going into haven't-washed-the-hair-in-days territory,' Sophie says to me, and it is her way of saying, *I'm not feeling great*. I interview my friend Helen for the podcast. She is also separated, and we compare notes on how far we could push our use of dry shampoo in those early days.

Six months after my daughter was born, the mums' group went out for dinner, our first night-time-no-kids-involved outing. I arrived first and, when the others got there, they didn't recognise me for a minute. I'd had my hair highlighted for the first time since having Sarah. Not that having a baby is a crisis as such, but it requires the same level of effort. Fripperies go by the wayside.

Working from home, I can get away with wearing mostly gym gear. In the aftermath, black Lycra had become my uniform. To leave the house, I step into my duvet coat, exchanging the sartorial shelter of the dressing gown for another almost floor-length piece. There was also a gargantuan black puffa jacket with a huge fur-lined hood, the closest thing I could get to actually bringing my duvet out into the world with me as a shield. 'You look like a Kardashian in that,' Sophie says at the sight of me swamped in this most outlandishly oversized of garments.

Clothes became a sort of armour to help me see out the worst times.

I can't remember when exactly that began to change, but, eventually, as I began to move away from the crux of things, there began to be room again for more than just the business of getting through. Life isn't just a struggle. The days aren't all exhausting. You get breaks in between that stuff. There is room for other things.

Having worked on fashion shoots for years, I have friends who are hair and make-up artists. Going to get my hair cut by Paul or coloured by James or my make-up done by Dearbhla was a way of being looked after for an hour or so by a friend, even if that friend knew nothing about what was going on at home.

It was so small a movement that I barely felt it at the time, but things shifted, got that little bit easier. There was room for more than just what was required for basic survival. I didn't really notice it until Sophie pointed it out to me. I was beginning to look after myself again.

I started to enjoy things I hadn't for some time. To enjoy dressing up. I bought five pairs of black high heels, all of which would have made me taller than my ex if he had been standing beside me. I would never have bought them pre-split.

Much later, I interviewed two women for a piece on Christmas after a loss. Both their husbands had died. On the first Christmas, both bought shoes. One, a pair of Ugg boots she gave to herself as the gift from her deceased husband. She described feeling safe, encased in their warm fluffiness. How she knew he would want her to have them.

The other marked her wedding anniversary several days after Christmas. That first year, she started a new tradition; gave her children to her in-laws and took herself off shopping. She does that every year now, and every year she buys herself a new pair of shoes.

That first year, she bought purple suede knee-high boots with flat soles. Now, several years later, she buys stilettoes, a sign, she said, of where her life is now. It seemed to me a sign of how far she had come, how strong she was now, that she felt able for the precariousness of stilettoes, where before she needed to be grounded by flat boots.

Now, coming out of the shadow of my own loss, I can't stop buying colourful dresses. It's a form of colour therapy, for a person who previously wore mostly greys, blacks, blues and greens.

Sophie muses aloud about whether an intervention is needed.

'Who even am I?' I say to her, a person who formerly wore all dark colours. But, of course, it feels like I'm just finding out.

Chapter 60

The Dinner Party

I decide to throw a dinner party. It feels like it is time to move to the celebratory side of life occasionally, rather than lingering in the getting through. The once-enjoyable things that had come to feel like chores are beginning to feel enjoyable again.

'Will you and Seb help with the cooking?' I ask Sophie, dispensing immediately with the notion that I will be anything other than front of house at this event. I may as well factor this in from the beginning. Sophie and her husband are professional-level food people. Whenever they come over, I seem to lose whatever small skill I have with food and they end up taking over, stepping in to make the gravy for the roast (Seb), or flip the pancakes, a baby still in her arms (Sophie).

After a separation, you have to relearn how to do certain things. Some of it can feel grim, at least to begin with. Sunday evenings on your own come to mind.

This isn't my first time hosting a dinner since my husband moved out, but it will be the first without people who are related to me.

I tell my friend Nikki about my plan. My husband and I had been big dinner party throwers. We had hosted a dinner party especially to set up her and her now husband. 'Do it,' she says, 'you used to love having people over, and your parties were always such fun.'

The flattery works.

Top tip: if you are planning your first dinner party after a difficult time in your life, do not leave the shopping until the Friday evening, the night before. Nothing is more depressing, more guaranteed to make you feel as if everyone else in the world is tucked up on the couch with a spouse, than the Lidl car park at eight o'clock on a Friday evening. It's end of days stuff.

When I arrive, there are some terrifying-looking teenagers hovering by the door who I imagine look like they might be about to mug me. Instead, they step in when the trolley I have put money into refuses to move, one of them quietly leaning over me and taking the handle and sliding it out from the chain, just as I start to wrestle so angrily I am in danger of toppling the entire row.

'What dessert are we having?' Sophie asks as we make our plans.

'Brace yourself,' I say. 'I'm going shop bought.'

She deems this statement not worthy of acknowledgment; it is decided that the division of labour will be Sophie on desserts, Seb on rice – apparently, he has a method – and I will do the main earlier that day. Sophie gives me a list of herbs, trying not to look horrified when I say that normally I just throw in some chilli powder.

My brother, my intended wingman, is sick on the night, so I am on my own and panicking, naturally, when the doorbell rings. 'This is the one time in your life when you cannot be late,' I have told Sophie, not actually expecting her to break the habit of a lifetime. But it's Sophie and Seb, not late but early, arms full of food and pots, shouting their heads off cheerfully. I want to cry at the sight of them, am all relief, gratitude, happiness.

Everyone piles in soon after. Never in your life will you less need to worry about whether people will turn up to your party; no one turns down a divorcee's first invitation. It's mostly old schoolfriends who know my house well, and they spread out quickly, make themselves at home. Open bottles of wine. Put coats upstairs. Sort the music. Make it easy for me.

'I like those wine glasses,' someone says.

'Wedding present,' I say, and we laugh without awkwardness because life begins to go on.

Chapter 61

My Women in Arms

The first argument my husband and I ever had was over healers, and their usefulness, or lack thereof.

'A healer?' I shrieked, and snorted down the phone with such derision that I gave myself a coughing fit.

The thing is that, until then, I had never really needed to be healed. I had had an uneventful, very lucky, very trauma-free life.

Life hadn't broken me, so there was no need to go looking for people who might help me to fix myself. The only time I had done anything of the kind was after my gran died, when a friend had insisted on setting me up with her healer. The whole thing had felt deeply uncomfortable. There was some shaking of rattles and spitting of salt, and I remember thinking how allergic my quietly Catholic grandmother would have been at what seemed like such amateur dramatics – although when the healer told me she could see I was an indigo child, which seemed to denote some kind of inherent specialness, I felt quite pleased with myself.

I'll take it, I thought.

And then, of course, my marriage fell apart and needed all the help I could get, so I began to build a veritable entourage of healers and wise women that was positively Kardashian in its breadth and scope.

'Adding to the retinue, are you?' Soph asks when I mention a woman I have met who is a yoga teacher. But alongside those who work at this stuff for a living, I sought out a tribe of women who had also been through something that had, for a time, broken them, and who had put themselves back together.

Women in arms.

'I'm so glad this happened to me, because of the person it has made me. Because of where I am now in my life.' People say this sort of thing all the time after a difficult period. I'm not sure I agree. I get it, of course. I understand. The need to reframe the horrible thing that has happened.

Turning it, by the sheer force of your descriptive will, from a random act of fate – proof that life will get out of our hands and there is nothing we can do to control it – to something over which you have, in fact, some control. Believing that this thing that happened was, ultimately, a good thing rather than that it was just an awful thing that happened – and, even worse, that something else awful might happen. The total randomness is terrifying, and much harder to live with.

But sometimes life *is* just awful. And entirely random. Bad things happen to us. Things we wish had never happened.

But while we can't choose what will happen to us, we hopefully get to choose, sooner or later, how we respond to it. We might get to shape that narrative, if we are privileged.

When your world as you know it falls apart, you need other women to help you make sense of yourself. They will tell you of the similar things that happened to them and you will see how they survived.

Pam is back for another visit, and we go out for dinner with another college friend, Bex. We do that turbo-charged catch-up that mothers of small children whose time for meet-ups is limited do, where you speed obscenely fast through everything that has happened since you were last all in a room together.

I can see Bex trying not to look shocked by the intensity of it all, of how much has gone on. 'You're doing so well,' she says in her gentle way when Pam has gone to the bathroom.

In college, Bex was always the capable one, the one who had got up and out and gone horse riding before the rest of us had even woken to begin wondering what food we would offer our hangovers. Who helped the homeless and kept up piano lessons. Who could do it all. But with an ability to not make the rest of us feel chastened by her greatness; we just looked on in admiration. It's a gift.

Her words are high praise. I am ridiculous. I preen before I know what I'm doing.

'I'm glad this happened,' I say, the words out of my mouth before I've even thought them through. 'Well,' I qualify immediately. 'I'm not glad that it happened. But I'm glad about the way it has changed me.' It's not just that. It's the fact that now, in stretches that each time seem to last longer than the last, I feel entirely happy with my lot. That once I stop examining my life through the filters of the boxes I am supposed to be ticking, and just thought, '*am I happy*?' the answer was more often than not, yes.

When my cousin Ciara's daughter was five, she got lost in a shopping centre. Ciara was walking through the crowd with her three children lined up behind her – 'like little ducks,' she says now, smiling at the memory.

They stopped in a sports store to get shorts and, when she turned around, her eldest daughter was gone. For seven minutes, she was gone. Lost.

My cousin ran to a security guard, who put it out to his network, and the child was spotted by another guard. A family had seen her, she was crying, like her mother had told her to if she ever got lost; to cry, and people would know she needed help. The other family knew something was wrong.

Late that night, my cousin rang her sister, the psychologist. The cousin I ring every couple of months to ask a variation on the question, 'Is my daughter OK through all this?' To which she invariably responds with a version of, 'Yes. You're both doing fine.'

Sometimes you need a professional to reassure you. Having one in the family is a lucky break.

'Caoimhe got lost in a shopping centre today,' Ciara tells her sister now. 'She got lost.'

'No, Ciara,' her sister says. 'Caoimhe got found. That is what you tell her. She got found.'

This is the story my cousin tells her five-year-old. 'You did the right thing. You did what I had taught you. You cried, and people knew you needed help. And you got found.'

It is the outcome that matters. If you get to shape that outcome, to mould your narrative into a happy one, then you are lucky.

These women I search out are not broken. They are mended.

They are not lost. They are found.

Chapter 62

Conversation With Friends

I remember in our twenties having a conversation with two friends whose parents were separated. They were both worrying about their parents' welfare in a way I would never have dreamed of doing about mine. And I realised it was because their parents were all single and didn't have an each other. They were exposed in a way mine weren't.

My daughter was young enough when we separated that for her, it was her normal.

But in terms of helping her to handle it, what did occur to me through everything was that the best thing I could do for her was to make my own life proof, should she ever need it, that I was happy and very fulfilled. I try to show her this in as many little ways as possible. Ways that she will soak up by osmosis.

'Where you going, Mommy?'

Out with Sophie. To the book club girls. To visit Shereen. Coffees with Lewine. To interview a particularly interesting woman.

I tell her all of these things so that if she should ever look back, she will know how surrounded I was. And how much fun I was having.

Of course, no one can future proof anyone else from worrying about them. But as much as I can, I try to make my life such that she needn't worry.

Chapter 63

In Which I Become a Joiner

It turns out that different seasons present different challenges in the effort to get used to living by myself. In the dark and cold, you have no one with whom to hibernate. But, at the same time, you feel like the rest of the world is also hibernating, so you're not missing out on much.

Come the spring, and a bright evening spent in alone has the ability to render you convinced that the rest of the world is otherwise engaged, out enjoying beer gardens, beach walks, impromptu barbecues and picnics.

As the evenings begin to get longer, I feel myself get fidgety. My daughter goes to bed and it is no longer enough to lie beside her in the dark reading my book, or to spend a few hours working.

My mother steps into the gap, suggesting I do a sailing course; she will provide all the babysitting necessary. She will stay in, so that I can go out. My father is involved in the local club, and for years has been trying to convince me to join what I still think of as his new hobby, even though he has been sailing for decades now.

He had first tried to get me to sail when I was a teenager. I was signed up for the course and sat in a room full of people similar to me in age but who had practically sailed out of the womb, hardy types who knew the intricacies of knots and each other. I knew no one and faked to my parents a fear of capsizing and being trapped under the sail that I did not actually feel in order to get out of it.

Now, it is my turn to be hardy, and I sign up for the week long course. I am that cliché in the wake of marital breakdown, a joiner. I don't mind though. There is something comforting about being away from my kind – married couples in their thirties and forties with young children. The sailing club crew runs more towards those in their fifties and upwards. Many are on second marriages. Or widowed. Or never married. Weathered, but past the point where the thing that does the weathering comes as a surprise.

They are relaxing company. It's peaceful to be around those who think nothing of a marriage having ended, who are neither shocked nor scared by it.

I ask Rachel if she will join me, and she agrees instantly, relieved, I think, that I have been distracted from threatening nights out in Club Nassau; I have taken to plotting a re-enactment of weekday nights out in our twenties to Eighties Night. Her little boy has taken to waking before five, so that's the last thing she needs.

I am to crew for a serious, committed sailor. In the heat of the moment, he keeps forgetting I am a beginner, and looks surprised when I have to ask what to do, which way to jump, what rope to pull. At the end of the week, there is a race on the Saturday morning, and he expects us to win against a boat of huge experience. Race day is bright but very breezy with choppy waters. Our vessel is small, just room for the two of us, and we bounce energetically over the tops of the waves. To keep us from capsizing, I have to lean my entire body out over the water, as perpendicular as I can make myself, weighing us down.

'You know they've got a marriage out of this course,' my mother says with a naughty gleam not unlike my daughter's. She herself has refused to take part – she'd had a brief foray that led to a lot of muttering about how couples should not sail together. Legend has it that one wife actually jumped ship mid-race, rather than remain in the boat any longer with her spouse, so heated had things become.

We win, and I see exactly why in in the aftermath of

an ending, people take up new things. The exhilaration of this new skill. I see my daughter standing at the wall with her grandfather, both waving excitedly, both wearing their matching white shirts. I can see she is a little baffled by this version of her mother, dressed in bulky waterproof gear, who jumps in the water and hauls a boat up the ramp. Always ready with a Disney parallel, she has announced that she will have her own boat. She is, of course, Moana in this scenario.

'It's a brain break,' Rach says one night as we queue on the slip waiting to go out on the water.

She's right. During the week of the course, getting out onto the water for two hours each evening and learning to sail, to steer the boat, jump out of the way of the boom, chasing other boats and looking back to the land and seeing it from a fresh angle lifts me out of my daily stresses entirely.

Chapter 64

The Safe Cross Code

It's the Easter Holidays and we've yet again hijacked one of Mo and Grandad's trips to Spain, blithely presuming without ever actually asking, that they are delighted to have us. My daughter and I are making our way slowly across the packed beach beside our apartment when I hear someone with a Cork accent shout my name.

I look up and see my friend Yvonne. We had worked together in the same building for years, she on the daily newspaper, me on the Sunday. She is one of those people with whom you assume an instant familiarity (or at least I do), in this case because she is Cork, and I do this to all Cork people because my mother is Cork, and because Yvonne is just like that. Straight, no bullshit. Full of definite opinions. One of my favourite kinds of people; a Cork journalist.

I had interviewed her for the podcast and now we have become proper friends.

She is on holiday with her husband and her two girls. My daughter knows her eldest and the two children get stuck in immediately, playing together in the sand, comparing LOL dolls. I sink into a sunbed beside Yvonne, and we get similarly stuck in. Talk about everything. Work gossip, raising daughters, she's just become self-employed and we discuss the terror of that versus the freedom with your children. We chat for hours.

We're now gate-crashing two holidays – my parents, and Yvonne's. They watch my daughter on an afternoon when I work at our apartment. Their eldest comes for a playdate and I get to read my book on the terrace while they play. We divide up snacks when one of us forgets to bring them or runs out. I forget my wallet and they include my daughter in their ice-cream run. I cook pizza at our apartment, bring it down to the beach and we all tuck in. She takes my daughter to the bathroom with hers, meaning I don't have to move from my sun lounger for another hour. Little things but huge things.

Chapter 65

The Grey Lady

The direct translation of my name into English means grey (Lia) and poem (dán). But its actual translation is the grey lady. When the boys in school heard this, they liked to endlessly pronounce it as dramatically as they could, teasing. It describes exactly how I feel some days. Out of nowhere I wake up and am a lead balloon, sunk to the bottom of a lake, watching my life through layers of murkiness. Whatever the weather is on these days it serves to compound the feeling. Overcast enhances how I feel. Sunny and I feel like I am letting my daughter down by not getting out there. But I need to shut my world down. Make it as small as my bed.

Chapter 66

Running Away, Part Two

'Are you awake?' Shereen calls softly from the other bed.

'No, I'm dozing,' I mutter.

'Same,' she replies.

'Amazing,' we both murmur, and go back to sleep for another hour.

It is spring, and we have run away together for the weekend, leaving our families behind. Running away when done by two mothers of several children under five is less like running away, and more like a mission planned with military precision, involving a team of people behind us at home doing the minding – co-parents, husbands, siblings, grandparents. It takes a village to replace a mother.

'How did the night go?' we ask each other both mornings, after texts from our respective families. When that is out of the way, we can relax, knowing that our children are not terrorising their relatives with middle-of-the-night floor pacing.

Set free from the tyranny of packing for small children, which generally leaves enough brain space for merely flinging together a few basics for oneself, we have both, rather bashfully, brought four bags. We decide to go for a sea swim – something Shereen does regularly, and something I talk about doing regularly.

Even though it is not yet summer, the sun is blinding but down on Inchdoney Strand, it is freezing.

'I can and I will and I want to,' Shereen says a friend of hers repeats to herself as she gets in for a sea swim.

I tear my clothes off, shove them in our bag and start running for the water, shouting the mantra.

'Wait for me,' she calls after me, surprised, I think, that I am actually going in this time.

If I stop I wouldn't start again so I keep running. It is freezing, agonising.

'Keep moving', we shout at each other, as waves roll between us. I flap my hands frantically, trying to warm them.

'Are you not putting your head under?' Shereen shouts across the waves.

'Can't. Contact lenses,' I say with as much of a regretful shrug as I can manage given my entire body is tingling painfully.

It's an excuse I've been trotting out since we were thirteen and at the Gaeltacht. They tried to make us do a capsize roll in kayaks, which I had decided was absolutely out of the question.

That evening, we go kayaking on a lake. The light dies as we are pushed out on the water, me at the back, steering.

'Have you kayaked before?' our teacher asks me, as he glides by. 'That's excellent steering.'

I spent the rest of the hour preening insufferably, directing Shereen, who *has* actually kayaked before, in oar manipulation.

It's remarkable what we can see without light pollution, the stars give us what we need. Our guide tells us to put our hands or oars in the water, and we raise a million tiny crackles of light. Phosphorescence. Unexpected magic.

Chapter 67

The Rest

The summer holidays were long underway and, contrary to all expectations, everything felt easier. I say contrary to expectations because I was not on holiday from work. And I do not have official childcare. And my family who usually helped with childcare have either had the temerity to take a holiday or were sick. But even though I was working, it felt different, in the way that a Saturday does from the rest of the week, even if you are working.

I decided there is nothing for it but to go with it. We go entirely off schedule.

My daughter has a superpower. Her true body clock runs something like nine in the morning to nine in the evening. Left to her own devices, she can sleep until as late as ten o'clock on rare, magical occasions.

We take the foot off the pedal. Don't set alarms. Go visit Nikki and her new baby. I finally bring my daughter for her last public-health check-up, two years late. 'She sees Dr P regularly,' I say in a defensive huff. 'It's been a difficult time.' (This works every time for getting out of awkward stuff.) The nurse smiles in amusement as she applies the tests for a two-year-old to a child of four.

It is hot and, in the afternoons, we loll on the couch, worn out, eating slices of melon cold from the fridge, watching cartoons, dozing. We go to the beach and the park, spend an afternoon at Sophie's where the only way we know what time it is is by the RTÉ radio schedule. We go for dinner at my parents' house, everyone bar my brother is away, and the three of us lie on a rug in the garden eating pizza. Meals are made up of whatever is easy and to hand. Crackers and raspberries, pasta and strawberries.

On Monday morning, we make pancakes, just because my daughter woke up and asked for them.

Chapter 68

The Anniversary

Sophie and I had spent weeks planning what we would do for my first wedding anniversary since the separation.

Not a date you ever plan to have to mark in your calendar, but there you have it. Last year, when we split, it was a matter of simply getting through. Of sitting outside my house in my car crying and booking a course in meditation. This year, we're attempting an itinerary. Partly distraction, partly to prove that this day can be more than something that just needs to be got through.

My friend Annie is hosting a yoga workshop in three parts. The first involves rolling around on a small hard ball, something like a hockey ball, enjoying that satisfying ache of stretching out tightened limbs. Sort of proof of how stressed you are, like when you go for a massage and ask the masseuse with relish if she's ever come across anyone with such knots. And you want her to answer no, that yours is the worst case of stress she has ever come across.

Then we do some yoga mixed with Pilates and, afterwards, we lie covered in fleece blankets for the guided meditation delivered in Annie's softly lilting voice. It's all women, about twenty of us, arriving in various stages of exhaustion. Some have come on their own, at the break everyone chats easily.

The early-September sun slants through the windows onto the bare brick and the grey painted wood.

Afterwards, Soph and I go to our favourite nearby Thai restaurant before the cinema, part three of the day.

We're getting settled in the dark cinema, spilling Maltesers into our boxes of popcorn, when the film begins. It's *Mamma Mia* 2. A beautiful Grecian beach, blinding sunlight and turquoise water leaps onto the screen.

'Oh shit,' I say. 'I'd forgotten. We went to Crete on our honeymoon.'

We had gone to the non-Leaving Cert side of the island (something we kept having to explain to people when they looked surprised at where we were going, and I knew they were picturing bars full of teenagers drinking out of funnels).

Two weeks of eating and sitting by the beach and the pool in our own private villa. At the first meal, exhausted from all the emotion of the wedding, I got drunk on the local wine and cried over the freshness of the tomatoes.

'You're going to feel a bit overwhelmed after the wedding,' Kate, one of the schoolfriends, and herself recently married, had warned me. 'I think it's from having everyone you love together and then suddenly they're gone.'

She had described feeling the odd need to always have her husband within her sight the first few days. During our stopover in London we went shopping and I panicked like a small child when I lost him in Topshop where I was pointlessly buying jeans that would never fit again after the honeymoon put an end to unsustainable wedding weight.

In the cinema, Sophie turns slowly towards me in the darkness, the blue light of the Greek waters flickering across her face as an expression of *eeeeek* spreads across her face.

'D'you want to leave?' she asks.

I shake my head. 'Nah. Let's see how it goes.' Leaving would seem like such defeat.

I haven't seen the first movie, but my mother and my daughter are big Abba fans. There are few things as enjoyable as watching a small child passionately belt out Abba's most plaintive numbers, you can hear them coming in my mother's car before you see them, Abba booming, the two of them singing their heads off.

Sticking with it turns out to be an excellent decision. Because this, more than anything, is a love story about a mother and her daughter. It's the only positive representation of a single mother I have seen on a screen bar the *Gilmore Girls*, which I have taken to watching obsessively in the past few months. When the ghost of Meryl comes on and sings 'My Love My Life' I can barely hold it together. Sophie looks over in concern.

'Happy tears,' I gulp, giving her a feeble thumbs up to which she looks unconvinced.

In amongst all the ridiculousness of the various men, it's the mother-daughter relationship that has the real clout. Identifying oneself with Meryl is ludicrous, it goes without saying, but watching her on the screen makes me feel my own life is validated. That this is enough. More than. And, like the *Gilmore Girls*, the movie shows what being a single mother is beginning to feel like to me. That beyond the exhaustion over the day-to-day and the fear over the future, the fact that the most important relationships of my life can be with the women of my life; my daughter, mother and best friends. There is something quite liberating about deciding that this is what my life is going to be, digging in to your reality. Especially when that reality is increasingly not, after all, something to be suffered through, but something to be easily enjoyed.

Afterwards, Sophie and I walk through the dark streets connecting Rathmines to Ranelagh, then stand beside her bike chatting for a half hour. The anniversary and the honeymoon are forgotten. We put a date in the diary, the first *Mamma Mia* will be our next movie night.

We have proved that this day can be something else.

Chapter 69

A Love-Hate Relationship

Sometimes, it is easier to hate the person you once loved than to remember how much you once loved them. Or if not hate, then maybe just forget. Repress the memories of them.

I see it in Sophie when I tell her an anecdote about her lovely father, at a time when he lies in hospital, all traces of who he was now long gone. She looks at me politely, humouring me in the manner of someone tolerating an anecdote about a person she does not know.

I recognise what she is doing. It is too painful to remember her father as he was before he got sick, so she has blocked it out.

Throughout all of this, I have only seen my mother cry once. She is not a crier generally, something that's been very helpful. When your life is falling apart, the last thing you need is to have to manage the sadness of others.

But one day in my kitchen, months ago, she broke down sobbing. She explains she had come across some photographs on her tablet from our wedding. She wasn't expecting to see them, they had taken her unawares.

Pictures of us leaning in to cut a cake, one of the many made by friends who had stocked and manned a desserts table for us. I had suggested to them, no doubt to their secret horror, that it might be a fun idea to do a homemade dessert table. The kind of thing you think might be fun when you're in the throes of wedding-planning insanity. Rather than giving your guests some damn dessert and letting them be.

'I forgot how happy you once were,' she sobbed.

It is easier to forget the way things once were. What you once had. To not think of the other person as the person they were when you loved them. Sometimes being angry at them or simply blocking them out is easier than remembering how you loved them.

You can think yourself into believing your marriage happened completely differently from how you believed it did. Become entirely disassociated from it. Tell yourself that this was always inevitable. That things were never quite right. Because, for a time, that is easier.

The loss is easier to manage, to tolerate, if you lie to yourself about what it is you are losing. You can pull at the loose string until eventually the whole thing comes apart.

And the anger can be sustaining. Much later, if you do get to the point where you figure everything out between you, where things settle, and all the anger evaporates, it is great, but it is difficult too. Because at the very least, for a few moments, you will just be two people who once loved each other very much, and who both love their child very much. So between the three of you there is all this love. And in how they are towards your child, you will see them as they were when they loved you. And for a moment it will feel so sad all over again, that things didn't work out. Without the anger to mask things, you see this, and have to absorb it.

Shortly after the anniversary, I interview Elizabeth Gilbert and she tells me she is finding the second year of grieving after her partner Rayya Elias died more difficult.

'I think it's because you're more able for it,' I tell her. 'As you move away from the combustion part, you're better able to comprehend the enormity of the loss. The shock and numbness is wearing off.' And then I immediately think, *Oh my God,* stop *advising Elizabeth Gilbert on emotions, you're embarrassing yourself. She knows this stuff. It's like giving Oprah life lessons.*

'You're not going backwards because you feel sad again,' Shereen tells me one day on the phone. 'You're going forward. Through.'

My friend Eilis, who lost her sister Lynn, says she loves talking about her, because she is afraid otherwise that she will forget. I prefer to forget. Divorce makes it hard to enjoy the memory of the good because, if you do, it is harder to reconcile that it is over but there they still are.

'Would you be interested in a piece about a divorce retreat?' I ask my editor, and she agrees. When I go to research it, I find a lot of screaming into desert-type resorts. Not at all what I'm after, I'm long past that part. I want white sands and turquoise water, with maybe a side of yoga.

A trip comes up with all of this, not strictly a divorce retreat, a private island in the Caribbean, all white beaches, clear water and coconuts in palm trees – essentially, the eighties Bounty ad. Sickening, I know. It is impossible not to sound smug whenever I tell anyone where I'm going.

We arrive and it is everything you might imagine. Except for me. I feel at odds with the world. Sadder than I have for months.

'You're in paradise for God's sake,' I tell myself. But I feel tainted by sadness, as if it sets me apart from the group. I start to refer to myself in my head as a divorcee, feeling slightly tragic and like a blowsy character who might be called Blanche and would be mostly half cut. I imagine the others in the group can almost feel the sadness emanating from me.

I am away from all the things that make my life nice, that compensate for the one big loss. My daughter, my family, my friends, my work. These are my buffers. Here, it is just me and my sadness. It scares me, how much of it is still there. I had no idea. I had thought I was so much further on than this.

In the early days after we separated, I had a time limit on how long I could manage on a night out before, out of nowhere, I would feel a wall of tears rise up in me, and I would know I had to leave as quickly as possible before they came pouring out. Usually it came from nowhere – one minute I was fine, the next full of tears which threatened to spill over.

This passed and I had forgotten it even used to happen until I get to my island paradise, and each night at dinner with the other journalists, I feel the tears well up in me again and I count time until I can retreat back to my bungalow. Tap my foot under the table, squeeze my hands together, like someone who needs to pee and cannot find a bathroom.

The loss hits me with the force of a sledgehammer. Not the details. The appendages. The future bigger family home, the future possible children, the blissful retirement or the family holidays we will not take. It is just the most fundamental loss that hits me. My person. He was once my best friend and I miss him.

On our last day on the island, I sit on a quiet stretch of beach all alone, counting the shades of turquoise in the water ahead of me, and think about how much I miss him.

Away from the people who have filled the gap, the loss feels almost fresh. On this deserted stretch of paradise, tears run down my face from behind my sunglasses. It scares me, how much grief is still there, unbeknownst to me.

Me, who has counsellors and healers and yoga teachers and crystal meditation groups.

It has taken me four days to realise why since arriving in paradise I have felt so upset. I have hit my plateau.

It comes up time and again in interviews for the *How to Fall Apart* podcast, 'the plateau'. You get through the worst part of the crisis by never stopping.

Stopping to think about things and take stock isn't possible, there is no time – and, anyhow, you can't; you're too raw, only fit for getting through.

When the worst is over, a little space opens up for more than just coping. That's when you need to get to the plateau. To give yourself a pause.

Not that this is always very nice. Because what tends to happen is that things crash in on you. It's when we loosen the vice-like grip on coping that we are maintaining in order to keep ourselves together, that sometimes things really hit. Which is scary and why we often put off experiencing the plateau and, instead, choose not to stop and look around.

'I'm not really sure that I am coping,' my friend Emily tells me in our *How to Fall Apart* interview, and admits that she hasn't taken a proper holiday in five years, since she had cancer, because she's afraid to stop.

It's why I'm sitting in paradise, crying my eyes out at something I thought I had put behind me. That's not to say that I thought I was all better and would never feel sad again. But I suppose I thought I wouldn't feel this specific type of sadness again. The sadness specifically at the fact of the break-up, that this has actually happened in the first place. I thought I had long accepted and moved on from that.

It feels scary, that all this could have been there and I had no idea. And then wearying, at the thought of yet another thing to be got through. But then it is got through and I feel better. Lighter, for not carrying around something I hadn't even realised I was carrying.

I'm at Malaga airport, on the way back from my Caribbean paradise. I hear her before I see her. I know exactly where to look, they are standing where my parents always stand in arrivals. There she is. She has jumped from her grandad's arms, ducked under the rail, and is barrelling towards me, leaping up into my arms, with all the aggressive affection of small children.

We squeeze each other. 'Mommy,' she whispers into my ear. Then, 'Present?'

After my marriage fell apart, it felt for a time as if my future had closed down. There was no hope or excitement, instead I looked to the future as a place full of gaping holes caused by the thing I had lost. I felt fearful about it, it was not a place I thought any good could come of.

Some things reawaken that hope, like new friends or new work. Some people make sure that that hope never really entirely goes away. She's old enough to walk but I carry her through the airport to where our car is waiting.

Part Three

Back Together Again

Chapter 70

In the Looking Glass

Pam and her daughter come to stay again. The girls, older now, are kept at bay with plates of strawberries and sausage sandwiches, distractions that quickly escalate into a box of craft supplies.

Being in Pam's company is a balm. She understands completely what it is to be a single parent – we even finish each other's sentences.

She knows the mixture of providing complete solidity for your child, while also feeling under the sort of pressure that might crack you open. She understands what it is to feel gripped by the fear of what this might be doing to your child, and to spread yourself as wide over them as you can, a sort of human tarpaulin.

Pam knows what it is to think of yourself as someone

who is generally on top of things, a capable person, but who now, sometimes, wonders how her life came to this. Knows what it is to be a person who can cope with a lot, but then experience one minor thing that seemingly involves the wellbeing of her child, and for that one minor thing to put you into a fight-or-flight panic mode you cannot get out of.

She understands the sadness that still hits occasionally at how far things have strayed from the life you wanted for your child, but I also see in her how much I am doing and how proud I should be of myself, because I see how much she is managing at one time, and I am so proud of her.

She knows what it is to rely on friends more than you would have without the separation, but to know that, at any time, they could disappear back into their family unit. That bank holidays can be tricky, because sometimes there is a limit to how much unstructured time you can handle when it feels like everyone else is engaged in familial barbecue bonding.

She knows the intensity of being a single parent to one child. The all and then suddenly nothingness of it, when they go to their father. To know what it is to try to fill those few hours when someone takes them. To be paralysed by indecision – prosecco brunch with friends? Gym? Meditate? Work emails? Housework? Stare at the wall? – and then to realise you're too exhausted to even make a choice and you've spent most of the time scrolling on your phone and watching bad TV.

It has been a hard week (month, really), when she comes to visit, the end of the holidays, and I am exhausted from patching together childcare while I work, but within half an hour I feel it all roll away.

We pass the weight back and forth, carrying each other. Switching from confiding to consoling within the length of an individual sentence.

'I know I'm not depressed, I just have the symptoms at times,' she says. 'But I can feel joy and I do look forward to things.'

'Situational depression,' I tell her, and then have to go check because I can't remember if it's something Helen told me or if I made it up myself, another self-diagnosis. Either way, I mean that this depression will pass because it is caused by your specific circumstances.

She recounts a story of a married male colleague, complaining about his workload – the number of emails, the having to work in the evening, etc. And we grimace at each other, and cackle with laughter, at this man who knows nothing of being the person who does the pick-up, the dinner, the bath, the putting down, then more work. This man who has a wife at home, picking up his pieces.

She understands how it is to love the individual men in your life but, at the same time, to feel a general sense of 'ugh, no thanks' at men. How a child proofs you against that because, when you are as busy as we are, it is hard to imagine giving up any of your free time to a new person, who might not even be worth it. If you are taking time off, it is to see your friends or family. People who are guaranteed to be worth it.

How when you have been forced to rely just upon yourself, it can become unfathomable to think of introducing another person into your home. Not just unfathomable, deeply unappealing. 'Why would you?' We laugh at the idea.

She understands how a good thing – a thing that was once lovely – can go wrong. And reassures me that it *was* a good thing, when I tear it apart in my head.

Later that day, I go to a lunch where everyone else is a married couple, and I think of Pam, hug the thought of her close, a buffer to feeling the loss too keenly amongst all these units of two.

She and her daughter stay with us for several days. At night in bed, my daughter whispers to herself, 'Bou and Pam, Lia and Sary. Bou and Pam, Lia and Sary.' The next morning, it is nice to wake to the sounds of others stirring in the next bedroom.

Chapter 71
The Things

There are things you think will always bother you, will always just slightly break your heart. They won't. When my husband first moved out, I thought I would always feel sad about the fact that my daughter wouldn't grow up in the home her father lived in. Specifically, I hated that he wouldn't be there for homework time. And then I realised that he wouldn't have been there for homework time anyway, he would have been working. So, it was a nonsensical thing to be grieving about.

But, also, time passed. I accepted our new reality. As I write this, there's a large cardboard box sitting open on a chair beside me. Inside are some toys. I'm packing them to go to her father's house, instead of to the charity shop. I was getting rid of them anyway –

having seen my friend describe on Instagram how she got rid of half the toys and how much more her two daughters played with that remained.

So, they were going anyway.

But if you had told me two years ago that I would be packing up some of her things to go to her father's house, and that it wouldn't bother me – that I would, in fact, be taking pleasure from this act of decluttering – I simply would not have believed you. I would not have believed that this would ever not be a sad thing.

The things you think will always hurt – they won't.

Chapter 72

A Home Away from Home

When you commit to someone, you place your sense of home within them. You might not do it consciously. It just happens. Grows upon you. A side-effect, almost. You are your real self with them – no side, no pretence, no outside social trappings. So being with them comes to feel like being at home.

They hold it within them, that sense of home. You feel at peace and easy in their company. Wherever they are, wherever you are with them, feels like home. Effortless.

They are your Friday-evening-turn-the-phone-off-get-the-takeaway-what-are-we-watching-no-one-is-asking-anything-of-you feeling. They are the place where you shut out the rest of the world, dial everything down, but are not alone.

So home is within them, but it is also out of them that you plan and later create your future homes – buildings and people. A family and a family's home. They are the very foundation stones of all the homes to come.

After the break-up of such a relationship, it is as if you have lost your home, even if you don't physically move anywhere. Because your sense of home had taken up residence – you thought permanently – outside of yourself, with them. No one goes into a marriage thinking, *Well, I'll keep a little bit reserved, just in case.* This may be something we do in other circumstances, for fear (rightly, probably) of losing ourselves. My intention is not to knock marriage, merely to point out that you cannot commit to it without losing a sense of yourself as an autonomous person. Marriage is the ultimate melding. I'm not talking about co-dependency here, but merely the planning a life together and agreeing to shared contours.

Maybe I am talking about co-dependency though. Marriage allows it. Marriage and motherhood; impossible to do without elements of dependency.

Even in a good relationship, you lose yourself. Or at least you commit fully to a version of yourself and how your life, at least in broad brush strokes, will be. Because going into a serious relationship with one foot in a different, imaginary, projected future is being an asshole.

'I think it is harder to lose a spouse than to lose a parent,' a friend who has lost her mother says to me one day at the park, as our children run around us, kicking a ball and collecting daisies.

And I know what she means. We expect, at least intellectually, to lose our parents. We do not expect to lose a spouse, at least not until life is almost done with us. Not while we are still in the midst of things, and so the losing them entails having to swerve dramatically from our intended course. To build a whole new way, homes we had built if only in our mind's eye crumbling.

When my marriage ended, I didn't move house, but other homes were taken away. The home that couldn't be seen but which I felt more strongly than anything when I found it, the home within my husband's person, and the future imagined homes I thought we would make together.

Parents are the home we come from, a spouse is the home we go to.

Past and future.

But, at the same time, flip the coin, and you will find that parents are elemental to the sense of yourself in a way a spouse isn't. We were never ourselves without our parents, they are there from the start.

In the office kitchen some months after my husband's mother died, a colleague asked after him. 'It's such a fundamental loss, to lose a mother,' she said quietly as we moved around each other in the small space, making the half-three tea. 'I think it took me years to even really realise, to accept, that mine was gone. I simply couldn't imagine the world without her.'

So even though it might seem unbearable at first, there was a you before them, before marriage. And so maybe it is possible for the losing of them not to be unimaginable. It becomes tolerable, and then just normal.

And, it turns out, there are other people who carry within them a sense of being your home. They do not always need to be a parent or a spouse. Cut yourself open, as the break-up of a marriage will do for you, and you will find, like the concentric rings within a tree, that you are more than just that relationship. That there are other homes within, and without you.

On any given day, Sophie knows what I am considering for dinner, the tricky email I am constructing a reply to, what my next deadline is, the outfit I'm planning to wear for the next night out. She knows what is upsetting me. What is making me happy. What's irritating me on Instagram. What I'm worried about. Whether or not I slept badly last night. Often, our phone call over breakfast is not our first contact of the day, which could have been WhatsApp messages from seven.

She is home.

Shereen is also home; friends since twelve. Rachel is home; lived together in our twenties. Nikki, now married to my cousin.

When my father goes away on holiday without us, as

he has the cheek to do from time to time, my daughter is always slightly bereft. Each morning on the drive to playschool, she asks how many days before Grandad returns, and we count down again on her fingers. Until it is time to go to the airport to collect him, she is ever so slightly unsettled. We video-call him every day – she props the phone up on her bedroom chest of drawers, pottering about the room chatting to him while she plays. I pass her door and peek in; she ignores him for large swathes, then shouts out an update as to what she is doing. 'Everything comes back to Grandad,' her playschool teacher tells me of the classroom chat.

He is a home to her.

Even though we now live under different roofs, her father and I are both her home. With the boundary-less, supremely unthinking presumption with which young children claim ownership of their parents' bodies, she makes herself at home upon both of us. Unconsciously plays with our hair, fiddles with our ears, throws an arm around a neck, jumps up on her father's back, barrels into our middles upon returning from an outing.

When her father sits, she often goes to stand at his knee, her arm slung around his neck, hand cupping his jaw. She hangs out of and slightly behind our legs on the rare moments when she feels shy. Her parents are her home. A boundary-less home. A moveable feast, but a feast nonetheless.

Chapter 73

Never Stopping

Right up close, it can be tricky sometimes to see that your life has fallen apart. Or is in the process of falling apart. Because if it is, then, chances are, you are doing everything you can to simply keep things going.

Feeding myself and my daughter. Making sure there are clean clothes, that the house is running, that bills are paid and deadlines are met.

And so, sometimes, you need to take a break to realise that things are not right. 'To look from a distance,' as Nancy says.

You're drained already by the weight of it all. Day-to-day life leaves no room for sitting back and reflecting. You need to take yourself out of it to assess, even admit, the damage.

I took lots of trips that first year. Now it feels like maybe there was a need to keep moving.

A few days in London, after things had been faced, but while it was mostly still just sadness and anger, a pause which felt like momentarily breaking through above water and being able to breathe again, and knowing that as hard as this felt, we were doing the right thing. And that the stress levels we had become inured to were not, in fact, normal.

A family weekend, an itinerary carefully curated over months by my mother for her seventieth birthday. A walk, a swim and a dinner. With people who knew what was happening, who gathered around me and my daughter. And despite being in the storm's eye, having a wonderful time. A sign that we would come out the other side, and things would feel complete, peaceful again, even if they would be so different.

A forty-eight-hour trip to Lapland with Sophie and Roo to cover it for the paper; two mothers and two children high on sugar. And realising that this is a person with whom I can manage a potentially highly stressful trip, and for it to be fun. Exhausting but fun. With whom I can weather a four-o'clock start with a three year old, jellies being thrown about with abandon by adult elves on the plane by seven o'clock, two toddlers fuelled by ginger biscuits and on the brink of Santa-proximity-induced hysteria, and that we endure it all and have fun, that it feels light, and like we are in it together. Sarah and Roo at bedtime cuddled together while Sophie read them a story. Friends who are family.

A weekend away on my own to Kerry for another work trip, a walk around the national park, and the feeling of heavy sadness, unexamined in real life, only beginning to be sensed, vaguely on the horizon, when I am away from it all. Sadness that will need to be dealt with eventually.

A stay at a lighthouse with Sarah and my parents, her excitement at being up close to such a structure. We, lifelong fans of Van Morrison, visiting Coney Island, which turns out be slightly disappointing. And I wonder at what my teenage self, who grew up listening to Van the Man, would have thought at the fact that her marriage would end.

A long weekend with Sophie at a bootcamp she is writing about for work. And the simple fact that exercising several times a day and being in nature makes you feel better. The handing over of responsibility and following the schedule they have created. And that none of these people know what is happening, and that Sophie makes me laugh even at the worst of times, and the knowledge that having a friend like that makes up for so much.

This summer, going on our annual holiday to my parents' place in Spain, the relief at having made it and excitement at getting on the plane with my daughter. Realising only from afar how much I have been contending with, and relishing the break from coping with it all.

'Extend your flights,' my mother urges, and we do. Sitting on the terrace watching her scoot by with her friend, they don't understand each other but they manage to communicate through LOL dolls. The other mother sitting outside her apartment on the other side of the pool, we know her from coming here for twenty years, she watches the children too, we share the responsibility. Long evenings on the beach where we eat takeaway spaghetti Bolognese and ice-creams, paddle and enjoy the emptiness of the beach after the busyness of the day.

A weekend with Sophie. Leisurely mornings unfettered by small children, hours reading, benefitting from Sophie's precise menu-planning. And in amongst the chat about friends, and their various house upgrades and pregnancies, a sadness settling, that these things are not for me. Sometimes, you need to give the sadness room to get in.

A work trip to London a few weeks into the new school year, when my daughter is settled, where I realise that, outside my comfort zone, I am much less fine at times than I might have thought. I am like Cinderella; undone by midnight, except instead I threaten to cry all over you. Exhausted by putting up a front, I leave the group of journalists abruptly, needing to dash back to my hotel room.

Chapter 74

The Single Supplement

I had headed off on my own to spend seven days in a cottage in Wicklow. It was a working trip but, in the absence of having to parent, it felt every bit like a holiday.

'I've gone into a coma of relaxation,' I say to Sophie in the first of my WhatsApp voice notes, dispatches from the outback. She will send me gossip and news from home in return. 'The moment I got into the car, I got this kind of clarity. I can do whatever I want.'

What do I want to do? Not much it turns out.

Actually, get out and go for a walk instead of telling myself each day I will and then failing to. Eat food my daughter wouldn't countenance. My week becomes a sort of passive-aggressive gourmand extravaganza.

Leek and thyme stew. Scrambled eggs drowned in tomato relish. Mackerels on brown bread. Cheese, tomato and spring onions on soda bread.

It feels wonderful. To be utterly free from any other person – friend, family or offspring.

I'm staying in the courtyard cottage of a beautiful old house, set amongst perfectly maintained gardens. 'Is there anything more calming than a well-tended window box, a border of lavender and a sash window frame?' I say to Soph on a voice note one morning.

'Do you need me to come down there with coffee?' she replies, concerned.

I watch videos of my daughter, as I do when I'm away and I miss her, but all I can think as I look at her in our home is, *There's that duvet in the background. I need to bring it to the dry cleaner* or *There's that bit of wall that might be damp* or *I need to work my way through that pile of paperwork.*

This may sound like a ridiculous level of busyness to lay claim to but even the cleaning out of our car had felt beyond me before I left. As I empty the door drawers of old popcorn bags and torn envelopes when I go down to the local shop/petrol station for supplies, I remember what Maureen Gaffney says in her book *Flourishing* about a messy car; a sign that your life is in some way out of control.

My house is lovely – and I am lucky to have it, of course – but, it's also occasionally feels like living within a to-do list. The exhaustion of running a house on your own as a single parent. Sitting in it is a reminder of the constant list of things-to-do-but-things-I'm-failing-at-doing.

As you do when you stay in a place that isn't actually occupied full-time and is therefore sparsely equipped, I start fantasising about the decluttering I will undertake upon my return home.

'I think I might have post-traumatic stress from the rat,' I confess to my mother on the phone, feeling ridiculous, as it was months ago. 'I've realised down here that I can't go into a room without banging on the door and rattling the handle first. Often, at home, in the evening I'll sneak up to the kitchen door and then burst in, in case there's one in there.'

'Of course you do,' she says briskly. 'I have it myself and I didn't even see the thing. Your father's bought those rat poison boxes and is putting them in the back garden.'

'I can't believe I haven't done this already,' I keep saying to myself about going away on my own, almost immediately afterwards realising that I probably wouldn't have been ready to do it before now. That, before now, instead of 'person goes off for week on own and relishes their own company like a pig in muck', I would have made it into 'now that my marriage is over I am off here on my own in a way I never would have been otherwise and no one else is having to go off on their own'.

Opposite my cottage is a golf course that was formerly the grounds of a big old house. I go for a walk dressed in four layers, like a person who has never actually been for a walk in their life; within minutes, I'm sweating and peeling them off until I have a skirt of jumpers and hoodies tied around my waist.

Most days the place is deserted, I see only the occasional golfer.

'I feel like I'm Marianne in *Sense and Sensibility*, tramping across the fields, with a dash of Roald Dahl from the pheasants,' I say to Soph on a WhatsApp message – quite clearly I'm high off my head on oxygen and from being surrounded by all the green. 'We should all just move to the country. We're mad living in the hurly burly of the city.' I'm sitting on the crest of a hill, taking in the surrounding hills.

Walking back down through the lane that is a tunnel of green, trees that join together high above me so I can hardly make out the sky, I feel like shouting with joy. Suddenly, my heart feels full of it. It rises up within me out of nowhere. That all is well within my world. Pure contentment.

Chapter 75

Can You Hear the Music?

A few months earlier, I wouldn't have managed a week on my own. Getting into my car to get onto the N11 would have felt like a sad thing. If my marriage hadn't broken up, I wouldn't have been going off on my own – and I'd have run through a list of people in my mind whose lives didn't allow for going off on their own. And thought that the fact that mine did was disadvantageous. A sign of things having come adrift.

I wouldn't have been able for it, for taking myself away from all the things that fill the hole. For such a comprehensive stopping.

My friend Nikki doesn't overthink things, she cuts through the emotion to the core of a thing, sees the clear way out of something. A helpful person to have when you are navigating your way through a divorce.

Whenever I am bogged down with things, I ring her, and we brainstorm it out.

'You think like a man, so unemotional,' I tell her and then immediately think to myself, *Christ the patriarchy really got to you.*

When things ended with my college boyfriend, Nikki and I were working together. I subjected her and Nancy to hours of plaintive songs in the boutique where we worked, which they tolerated grimly, but kindly. I see now that I was probably OK right from the beginning; no one who can listen to 'Landslide' and not be brought to tears is *that* upset. A year before my marriage ended, Nikki suffered a much worse series of losses. Afterwards, as she tried to cope, she told me that she couldn't go for the walks she used to love taking, because she could no longer listen to music – it was too upsetting – and she couldn't bear the quiet of nothing.

Later still, she confessed that in the really early days of her grief, she had found it hard to take a shower – even pausing for the two or three minutes, allowing her brain to stop, not occupying herself constantly, caused her to crumple.

She's started going for walks recently, three years later. Because that's what it's like when you're right up against a big loss. Stopping to contemplate it, pausing for a minute when that minute might reveal to you the extent of your pain, is terrifying.

Chapter 76

The Green Room

Back when I did the meditation course, I mentioned to someone how I craved green juices each day. Fixated on them. Drank three at a time.

'Oh that's your heart chakra,' they said. 'You're opening things up.'

In a guided meditation group some months later, when another woman mentioned feeling like there was a pane of glass between her heart and the rest of the world, my whole body jumped to attention in recognition of what she was saying.

It's hard to explain.

Since my marriage ended, in some ways, I've never felt so much love or so loved. My daughter and I tell each other we love each other daily, many times, and my family and friends, new and old, show it in how they have minded and supported me.

But when anyone asks if I want to meet someone, have another relationship, it's like again my whole body jumps again in recognition of something. 'Absolutely not, and unlikely ever to again.'

I want what I have.

I know that, somewhere within me, there's a block or a shut-down. If I wanted to get rid of it, it would be in the spirit of letting go of the past though, rather than inviting in anything new.

On my week's holiday alone, every day I cross the road outside the house to walk up the green tunnel. There's a wide, white wooden gate that before I touch it seems like it might not have been moved in years, so rotten it could fall apart in my hands, and then is surprisingly easy to move.

The path takes about fifteen minutes to walk, I imagine it is the old servant and trade entrance to the estate. The estate that is now a golf course but, most days, when I go for my walk, it is empty.

There is a walled garden with an orchard and, on the third day, I get caught in a rain shower and shelter there, the crabby tree branches knitted together above me keeping me dry. It turns out that squashing half-rotten apples beneath your feet is next-level satisfaction from bubble wrap.

A collection of pheasants accompanies me on

my daily walk. The first day, they burst from the undergrowth on the path up ahead, shocking me as I think they might be shocked by my presence. By day three, they potter along in front of me, pausing every so often to wait while I catch up.

The estate's house itself seems fairly derelict. There's a sort of end of days, Elizabeth Bowen's *The Last September* to it. Some windows around the back have been left permanently half open, there is a precise hole in one where a golf ball has shot through. The two rooms at the front, when I peer through the windows, are set with chairs in lines, as if for a long-ago concert. Out front, a row of cheap white plastic garden chairs, gathered along the side of the house beside the door, strike a jarring note.

Even though I know the car park lurks just somewhere over there, and I occasionally turn a corner to find a game of golf in full flow, the place mostly feels deserted and forgotten, as if only I know of its existence.

It feels as if I have never been surrounded by so much green in my life. All shades, all tones, and all sizes. Ferns are everywhere at my feet, always an instant hit of dopamine; a reminder of family walks as a child.

Back down through the green tunnel. I turn just before the gate to have a last look and, out of nowhere, without forming it or intending to, the words *thank you* float up in my mind. I am saying thank you to the trees. I know, its sounds mad. But I feel like they are giving something I didn't know I badly needed. Peace of mind. And something that feels like healing.

The next day, as I walk up the path to what I am now thinking of as my private estate, I go off the lane and into the woods. A feeling rises, of a presence. As if the trees are watching me. I know how mad this sounds, but when you feel something that you've never felt before, just because it sounds mad, doesn't make it not have happened.

The next day, halfway up the path I glance up and there's a large deer emerging from the trees. It pauses and looks back at me, before diving into the other side of the forest. Another day, again I get that sense of being watched, and when I peer through the trees, there is a deer watching me, we look at each other for a few seconds before it bolts again.

'Green is your favourite colour, Mommy,' my daughter tells me.

'Because it's the colour of my baby's eyes,' I tell her. I bring her to the optician, and she says her eyes are green, and hazel. Her mother, and her father, I think. 'Grazel,' the optician says, and I nod in agreement. Both of us are there.

On a job a while ago, a woman separated longer than me had remarked that being a single mother prepares you for empty-nest syndrome; that when your children go to their father, you get a taste of the future. I never had that thing mothers sometimes get of missing my old pre-child self. But sometimes I worry about my future self. For I am rebuilding my life with a person who changes all the time and who will eventually (as is right), up and leave.

So maybe this is to say that whenever I did stop, what I needed was offered up to me, when I lifted my head and looked around. Whether that was a friend shouting my name from across the beach, a quiet strip of sand on which to cry my eyes out or a parkland all to myself in which to realise there is nowhere I would rather be than right there, on my own, with myself.

Part Four

Things Fall Into Place

Chapter 77
Two Years On

Calling a section of your book 'Things Fall Into Place' seems like an extreme form of tempting fate. Like telling people the first time your child finally sleeps through the night; an almost sure-fire way to guarantee that it will not happen again for months. Or writing articles about grief having passed, only to find that almost the very next day would be a grief day. I have done both. And I am not here suggesting that things fall into place indefinitely. A happy ever after, full stop.

'Is it all depressing or happy ever after?' someone asked me just before Cassie, my podcast producer, and I put out our first episode of *How to Fall Apart*.

'Neither,' I said.

Because life is neither.

Chapter 78

First Day

My daughter is starting school and people keep asking me how I am. I know what they're getting at. I should be nervous. Overwhelmed maybe. Emotional definitely. But I am not. I'm fine.

Partly it is because I have intentionally set out to future proof myself against the upset. To be as calm and as balanced as I can, for her, as well as myself.

For both of us.

For the past week, I have gone back to meditation with a vengeance, if such a thing is possible, and I can feel it working. Creating that little well of happiness within me, formed by the daily meditations, and then felt more keenly for dipping back into it so regularly (twice a day, if possible).

Meditation brings everything down so that you feel less jangly and then, afterwards, there is the memory of that little oasis of calm which you can return to anytime you want to in your mind. Taste again the feelings of buoyancy and peace.

It reveals what is there, lying dormant within you, but if you've cleared out all the difficult stuff (for now, anyway), increasingly what you get is a small well of joy within that bubbles up for the rest of the day. I am ready to be happy. To feel calm, secure in our life.

Settled.

In the early days after our marriage fell apart, I would meditate and inevitably fall asleep. Because a deep, bottomless pit of exhaustion was what lay within me. A well of tired sadness that would come up and overwhelm me. And meditation revealed that actually what I needed was sleep.

Now, it feels like bubbles, floating up from within. Lightness. Buoyancy.

So partly, it's that. My calmness is thanks to my future proofing.

But it's also this. The last time we were at this rodeo – starting playschool rather than big school, we had just separated. I write that now and it is shocking. To think that I had to deal with that while facing the daunting task of settling a child in playschool at the same time.

'How's she getting on?'

'Oh fine, and by the way my marriage is falling apart.'

Back then, a run-of-the-mill morning drop-off could affect my entire day. So many pressure points to be triggered, so many things to compare myself and my own life to, all capable of being summed up under the title 'Perfectly Happy Families'.

'When she gets to school, half the class will be from separated families, it will be no big deal,' a teacher friend told me. And it was grimly comforting, but on a morning dropping her off, if my mood was there to be turned, wobbly, already faltering, the sight of others, living apparently unfractured lives, could be enough to sour a day.

Not now though. Contentment creeps up on you, and it's only when you are thrown into something new that your life is shown in relief and you realise the nature of its fabric. I am content. And if not bulletproof, largely immune to the poisonous arrows of self-comparison. I'm insulated from it in part by my own network of women, which tells me that behind the seeming calm or the 2.4 or the whatever it is I might have chosen to torture myself with, they – we – are all dealing with something. And I am insulated now by my own happiness in our life. Our movie nights and pancake breakfasts, our evenings while I work at the dining-room table and she plays beside me. It's domestic bliss, just not as you know it.

So, the sight of other's home fronts now rarely has the power to fracture my own sense of wellbeing. This is us. We are settled into things now. We are not fractured. We are remade. I don't mind about the situations of others.

We walk her to the school gates on the first day, her father and I. I calm her when she cries and I know we are all able for it, and then we leave and I am fine. We go to pick her up, and through the window there she is in the queue, jumping in excitement and waving. And I want to punch the air triumphantly. But if she had been upset, I know I would have handled that too. I would have coped. I would have been calm for her. Not pretending. Really calm. Because this does not phase me.

'I'm not saying a marriage ending is a good thing,' I say to Soph, 'but it's quite satisfying to know you will bend but not break.'

'You know that's Pink you're quoting there,' she replies.

'I'm glad this happened to me,' people say in the aftermath of difficulty. 'It made me stronger, put me on the path, made me the person I am supposed to be.' I get why they're saying it. Control the narrative. Put a good spin on it. And often they do feel the better for it. But to be able to say this is also to be in a position of privilege. Things turned out well for you, if you can say that. Nobody died. Nobody was irreparably hurt.

I don't say I'm glad this happened. Even though I am probably happier, because I have worked hard at it, so it is a different kind of happiness. Grown from within, rather than bestowed from outside. To say I'm happy my marriage ended seems somehow disrespectful. To my marriage. To my daughter. But the simple fact is that good things do come from this kind of thing.

For one thing, sadness would have scared me before. The sight of my daughter being sad would have terrified me, I would have felt it necessary to chase away her upset right that instant. Now, I can calmly tell her that everyone feels sad at times, it's normal, and the feeling will pass. And I know she can see that this doesn't faze me, where before I would have helicoptered anxiously around her, trying to make everything OK.

If you have weathered the storm of a marriage falling apart, then, well, not nothing else, but lots else, does not faze you.

That big loss buffers you from the smaller stuff. And it means that the things that really affect my sense of wellbeing, my peace of mind, are mostly only the big things. The wellbeing of my child being the biggest of the things. (Side note: I do not buy that idea of martyr motherhood. If my child is well, then chances are I'm well. This is not me not putting myself first. My child is the most important thing to me. I get a sense of wellbeing, from her being content. That's not sacrificing myself. If she's OK, I'm OK.)

My daughter takes to school. On the second day, a new friend hugs her hello as we wait by the gate. She is made leader of her table, an act I take as a sign that her teacher has spotted signs of incipient greatness. And while I could have handled it if she didn't take to it, and I know that a few days in doesn't a smooth road guarantee, the sight of her coming running out, smiling is a relief, as is the moment at bedtime when she tells me she had a lovely day. It feels like we are a balloon loosened from its string and floating off into the sky.

Above it all. Pure happiness, untouchable.

Chapter 79

The Last September

I had said to Soph early in the week, 'It's my wedding anniversary this weekend, we must plan something.'

It's the second wedding anniversary since we split, marking two years of separation.

'Movie night and the first *Mamma Mia*?' she replies instantly; we still haven't gotten around to watching it.

The week gets busy and we forget. I forget, in fact, until I'm halfway through the morning of the day itself.

When I do remember, it slips in gently, rather than as the painful crash it might have been the year before.

By then, my daughter and I already have plans.

We're meeting friends, Anna and Evie, a mother and daughter, at the park. As always on the first, it's a classic golden day. We get to the park and Anna offers to take the children and get the coffees while I go pitch our rug. I'm halfway across the park before the words are fully out of her mouth, delighted to have a few minutes to myself to sit in the sun.

There's a family opposite from where I sit, two parents, two children. They're unpacking an actual wicker picnic basket, cutlery and crockery are coming out from little strapped slots. *Surely tempting fate*, I think, observing this grab for perfection. Sure enough, five minutes later, both of the children are running amok, the older with a stick, riding about like a pony, terrorising everyone near him by jumping on them. His parents are screaming at him to come back. 'Adaaaaaaam, calm down, come here'. The neatly set rug has been thrown in disarray, and you can almost hear their inner monologue. 'For fuck's sake, Adam, stop ruining everything.'

I see Anna and the two girls coming back with supplies, mine galloping across the green towards me, I can see from here she's a unicorn pony.

'Neeeeigh,' she carols when she gets to me, a quick nuzzle of my neck just so I am in no doubt of what she is, then off to sit under the tree with her friend. The two of them munching on their banana bread and ogling the outdoor yoga class that is downward dogging beside us.

Anna and I lie out on the rug – it's still warm enough for us to all be coatless. I remember again that it's our anniversary. I don't bother to bring it up. Today is not about that. I thought it always would be, and yet, here we are, just two years in.

Chapter 80

The Woman From the Future, Part 2

I am sitting on the couch, watching Netflix on my own with casual abandon; the sight of an empty evening holds no fear for me now, when a WhatsApp message pops up. It's from an old work friend who I haven't heard from in six months.

'So … I've been getting some comfort from your column of late …' the first message reads.

'Is everything OK?' I text back.

'Joining the club,' she says, with a fearful-looking emoji face.

They are separating. She's just beginning to tell people. She tells me she's read the column on how to tell people. 'I'm not sad. I was so miserable for so long, I feel relieved,' she continues.

We decide we need to discuss things over a drink.

She texts again the weekend her husband moves out. I advise her on it. Talk to her about how it will be for the next few weeks. In the middle of our back and forth, I realise I have become the woman from the future.

Chapter 81

Doing it Anyway

It's so hard to make a living as a journalist because journalism is dying/There is no security in freelancing, but freelancing is this thing that gives me flexibility with my daughter, which is the most important thing to me/And my work is one of the things that makes me happiest/What if I lose that work? It's so hard to make a living as a journalist, etc. etc.

These are the fears that circled around and around in my head when I was tired or stressed or simply because I am getting a divorce and life is anxiety-making. A separation makes you constantly second-guess your life. Pull at it, judge its sufficiency. Will I be OK? Am I doing enough? Have I hurt my child?

It's exhausting.

My interview with Elizabeth Gilbert happens almost two years after we separated. As someone who writes a column about putting life back together after a marriage falls apart and your life goes off-piste, well, you can imagine my excitement.

For weeks beforehand, I peppered her publicist, a deeply patient man, with emails. 'Just checking in we're still OK for the twenty-third? ... Just wanted to confirm it's still alright for Cassie to record it for the podcast.' He responded by going so far as to arrange a private suite for us to record in. Truly a lovely person.

Afterwards, as we left the room, I remember Cass saying to herself, 'That's really good, what she said about fear.'

At the time I was too busy galloping joyfully down the hotel corridor, leaping up and punching the air every couple of steps, to notice what she was saying, but it came back to me afterwards.

What she had said was that the more you fight fear, the stronger it makes it. Better off accepting it as an inevitable. Then going about your business.

There is a crack in everything, that's how the light gets in, as the Leonard Cohen quotation goes. And it's true, but so is the reverse. When there is a crack, that's how the fear gets in. And the stress. And the anxiety like nothing you've ever felt before. It oozes in through your broken self, sets up home, where before there might have been no vulnerable spot through which it could break in.

Your system is working in such overdrive that things it might previously have almost unconsciously brushed off make their way in and come to seem like genuine, valid things to be concerned about. I worried about our steep wooden stairs. As if my husband, in retirement, would have carried me down them. But this seemed like a real concern, worthy of time spent thinking about.

But that is what separation, or any loss, does to you. For a time, the sense of the future as a place that is largely safe and not a matter for your concern shuts down. The future becomes something to dread, or fear.

To use modern parlance, you're in a constant state of being triggered. Your own life is a trigger, the sight of it, all broken to pieces, means you are in constant fight or flight. Staying buoyant is such an effort, anxiety easily gets on top of you.

First you look outside of yourself to assuage that fear. Eventually, you find the relief within yourself. The fear will always be there. If you spend your time fighting it, that simply serves to rouse it. Fuel it. Accept its presence, acknowledge it, *Oh yep, there you are, fear again, naturally*. When you accept that it will always be there, it is part of the nature of things, somehow it takes the sting out of it. It takes the terror out of fear, so to speak. There will always be fear, you think. Then you get on with it.

'Imagine you are standing in the water at the beach, holding an inflatable ball,' my cousin-the-psychologist says. 'If you try and hold that ball under the water, you may manage to for some time, but inevitably it will burst up above the water, and either hit you or at the very least cause a splash that will hit you. Pushing against it merely serves to increase its momentum. Instead, let that ball sit beside you. It will go out with the tide, but inevitably it will come back. Always there, at some times more felt that others. Occasionally it might brush against you. But by accepting it, it won't hurt you as much.'

'I think I'll have to look at a new career. Give up the journalism,' I said to my mother one day, in deep fear.

She looked at me blankly, as if I was talking a language she didn't understand.

'It's simply too risky. There's no security,' I continued.

'Yes, but it's working out right now?' she asked pointedly.

I nodded.

'And you love it? It makes you happy. And you're doing the kind of work you love. As if you've found the right path for you?' Which for my pragmatic mother, is a very woo-woo thing to say.

She was right of course. Giving up something I love and which brings me great joy for fear it might, in the future, not work out is absolute nonsense. Work gave me a new future to feel excited about at a time when the one I had planned fell apart.

Chapter 82

The Red Tent

Put women in a circle and things start to happen. A book club, a work collective, a mothers' support group. My friend Dawn hosts a workshop for single parents. Ten women sit in a circle. What begins with the intention of being a quick spin around the group so we can each do a short introduction takes most of the allotted time, as each woman offers up her story, and the others respond with empathy, advice and support.

Lou tells me about the concept of the red tent, a domain into which women would have retreated for about seventy-two hours when they lived in communities, and their monthly cycles were synched, in which to rest, retreat, but also to access the realm of the spiritual. 'The realm of the unseen,' Lou says.

The women would support each other, listen to one another. A safe space.

'Can you even *fathom* what your life would be like if you did that every month of your life from the age of twelve?' Lou says. 'It was task-less doing.'

Afterwards, the rested and connected women went back to the tribe, and anything they would have considered or meditated upon would then be delivered and be taken on board.

'We have this deep, introspective programme running in our bodies, and there's some real gold to be found there, if the conditions are created,' Lou says. 'I would call it the spiritual. It's what I would call source power. The animating force behind all phenomena. If I was to give it a gender, I would say it's a mother. Sometimes, I would say Great Mother.'

'We are not in the business of fixing ourselves. We are in the business of accepting ourselves,' Lou says.

Chapter 83

Back in the Room

I go back to Helen one last time. More for a check-up than for anything specific. When I walk into her room it has been entirely denuded of everything bar the three chairs; Helen's more upright wooden framed seat, and the two armchairs facing her, where my husband and I had sat, beside each other, but really so very far apart, that first time we came to see her. 'Are you painting the walls?' I ask nervously.

'No,' she replies, 'moving office.' *Please never retire*, I want to say. But I know that this is our last session, for now anyhow. It feels more like a catch-up with a friend that a counselling session; I fill her in on the past few months, she asks after my daughter.

'I'm only up the road,' she says with a smile as I'm getting ready to leave. 'Should you ever need it.'

And I leave. And he's not with me, I'm on my own. And I want to thank her for helping me to be alright with that.

Chapter 84
Surrounded

'The new *Frozen 2* posters say to let go of the past,' I say to Sophie, pointing at them as we leave the cinema, where we've just seen the movie with the kids for the first of no doubt countless times.

'Elsa speaking to you again, is she?' she replies.

'There she is, surrounded by the four elements,' I say of what we've just witnessed.

'Are you about to cast yourself as Elsa in your book?' she asks suspiciously, with a stern raise of the eyebrow.

'Perish the thought,' I reply quickly. 'If anyone is Elsa in this story, it is my daughter. Although she is more of an Awwna really. Able for fear, and so much fun.'

It's just that I felt surrounded. Women who caught, helped and propelled me. Navigators.

I don't know that I would describe myself as a spiritual person. That might be the vestiges of a reluctance to take on anything that feels like religion, for wanting to make the point that to be non-religious is more than enough. And, frankly, from a reluctance to be a part of any club that would not have me as a leader.

But I suppose if spirituality is considered an awareness of, and a subsequent ability to rely upon a sense of something that is larger than ourselves, or outside of ourselves, something that supports us, then I am on board. I like the AA notion of spirituality; one that is self-defined. A higher power we name individually for ourselves that can be in and around us.

'I am stronger when I'm with other people,' Lou says when I ask her what spirituality means to her. 'I would believe spirituality is inherently good, and, if there's a word or a principle, it's love. The vibration of life is love. It's the heart and nature and connection. You're in the realm of the spiritual when you're in your heart. You're in the realm of the spiritual when you're in nature. You're in the realm of the spiritual when you're in connection with other people. Other women.' So spirituality can be a sense of connection, actually a comfortingly tangible thing for a non-believer.

And spirituality can be a sense of faith, and your faith can in part be a belief in the safety of your world. Faith in the people around you, that they will catch you when you fall.

'Who is in the centre of your ten circles?' Maria asked.

It is my daughter and I. But all about us, in the invisible concentric circles which surround us, are our people.

Chapter 85

How to Find Your Way Home

The day I get offered a book contract, I come out of the meeting with my editor and am hit by a wave of sadness that I am not ringing my ex-husband, once the first person I would call with such momentous news. It still has the power to shock me sometimes, that he is gone from my inner circle.

But that's what it is. Not black and white. Grey areas. 'A divorce is like a death without a body,' Alan Alda says in *Marriage Story*, and it's one of the truest things ever said on the subject.

Because you do not shake off someone who was once fundamental to you that easily. A person who, when you met them, felt like finding home. It's like a death; on those big days, the loss is always there, hovering just at the edge of your line of sight.

Mostly though, the further away from the catastrophe you get, the easier it becomes. But just occasionally, as the memories of the heat of the combustion and all the pain of that, and the relief that that part is over, fade to a distant memory, there is a different, softer kind of sadness about how things have gone.

Soon after, I go to New York on a work trip. I had forgotten that the last time I was there, we were celebrating my thirtieth birthday, ten years ago. We went to Balthazar's for lunch, took in a cheesy open-topped bus tour in what we assured each other was an ironic way, and tracked down what claimed to be the world's best red velvet cake in a small restaurant at the docks, hidden just behind the skyscrapers.

I see our younger selves on every street corner.

It was my husband's first time there and he couldn't get over the city. We had planned to come back every year but we never did. It hurts in a way that I hadn't expected, and I feel all over again that sense of being raw and exposed that is grief, the self-consciousness of it, as if everyone can see right through me. I put on my sunglasses, stare fixedly out the window, and hope that my fellow journalists won't notice that I'm crying.

On the last day of our trip, as we wait on the subway platform, two of the other journalists and I have a conversation out of nowhere about loss and grief. In amongst the whistling wind that flies through the tunnel and the barrelling of trains, it feels as if no one can overhear us, and with these two almost-strangers, there is an unexpected moment of total honesty, where we all know what we have gone through, and I feel better again and not alone. Later the three of us go for a cycle through Central Park and, for that hour, it feels like we have bonded by the simple acknowledgment that everything is not always OK. The weight I had felt of the sadness comes off.

Second-year grief sadness.

As the images of the hard parts at the end fade, memories of the lovelier bits earlier on appear in their absence.

At times, I still have to find the spot on the stairs from where I am invisible to the outside world, where I would sit and cry, suddenly overcome, dashing from my desk, but these days if I cry it is mostly because a sudden, overwhelming relief comes over me. I did it. I kept us afloat and then I rebuilt. And it is the thought of the people who supported me. All that love. And of my little girl, a person around whom to build a life, that overwhelms me.

Sometimes, when I write about my daughter, I worry that it might be hurtful for others who don't have a child and might want one. But the thing is that, up close, we are all missing pieces. The lovely husband. The calm father. The supportive mother. The joyful child. The best friend who is a sister-wife. All you can do is to have as many pieces as possible to your jigsaw. To weave the net underneath you with as many different threads as possible.

I ring my mother, then Sophie, Shereen and Rachel to tell them about the book. There are tears and screaming. Jumping up and down in the middle of Penneys. Rachel tells me she is proud of me, and proud is something you can only be of someone you're claiming a stake in. In whom you have a sense of ownership.

I go home to my parents' house to tell the rest of them and, as I get to the door, the memory of another time I arrived at their door with big news flashes before me. I hadn't intended to tell them then, that I thought my marriage was over. My brother was arriving home from China, and I didn't want to take from my mother's excitement, which had been building for weeks. But they opened the door and I burst into tears, because sometimes the mere sight of your mother undoes you. Makes you stop, unable to hold it together, whatever your intentions. Wordlessly they stepped into the breach with perfect synchronicity; my father reached out and took my daughter, who was oblivious to my crying, and headed left into the kitchen. My mother went right with me into the living room.

Now, it feels wonderful to have something to bring back and drop at their feet that is not crying or stress, but a reason to celebrate, having felt for some time like our family cat when it would bring unwelcome gifts of dead mice to the back door.

'I have big news,' I say.

They sit in a line along the couch, Mo, Grandad, my brother and Song, looking at me expectantly, my mother trying to disguise her excitement because she already knows.

'Is it a present for me?' my daughter grins from the doorway.

I tell them, and then I burst into tears, and they all jump up, and jump around cheering, dancing half out of excitement, half to conceal from her my tears.

'Don't let her see you crying, well done,' my mother whispers in my ear.

'She won't understand the news,' I had thought earlier as I drove to my parents' house. But I'll tell her I'm writing a book about love, for her, and I cannot wait to to tell her that.

We will dance our hallelujah dance, our arms in the air. It is our dance for when we are excited and celebrating, first started when I lost my bank card and scared the hell out of her with my cursing and blinding before I located it in my other handbag, so then compensated with a ridiculous dance. And then we will treat ourselves to a Bombay because it is Friday, and we have things to celebrate.

I cannot wait to get home to her. For she is home.

Acknowledgements

Writing a book this personal can be terrifying at times. Having an editor you trust implicitly makes all the difference. I am hugely grateful to the brilliant Ciara Doorley for her advice, guidance and always-spot-on feedback. Similarly, to my fantastic agent Sallyanne Sweeney for her support.

To the wonderful Anne Harris, who asked me to come write for her at a time when I was too shy to show anyone anything I had written.

To the hugely supportive Mary O'Sullivan, Brendan O'Connor, and Constance Harris, all brilliant editors who taught me how to be a journalist.

To Laura George for commissioning the 'Things Fall Apart' column, and to Dominique McMullan, Grace McGettigan and Erin Lindsay.

To the team at Hachette Ireland who have worked so hard creating this book, particularly Elaine Egan and Joanna Smyth, and Madeline Meckiffe for creating such a beautiful cover.

To my colleagues at the *Sunday Independent, Image* and *Irish Tatler*, especially Chloe Brennan, Gemma Fullam, Jane Doran, Cormac Bourke, Madeleine Keane, Fran Power, Kip Carroll, Sarah Macken, Lizzie Gore-Grimes, Meg Walker, and my *rogue* collective crew.

To Cassie Delaney, the woman who can do everything. Thank you for agreeing to make a podcast with me.

To all the women who have so generously told me their stories on the *How to Fall Apart* podcast, in particular Mary Greene, Yvonne Hogan, Eilish Downey, Nadia Forde, Helen Steele, Kate Gunn, Emily Hourican, Ellie Kisyombe and Elle Gordon for their ongoing friendship and support. And to everyone who has listened to *How to Fall Apart*.

To Teresa Daly for early advice and Nicola McEnroe for technical know-how.

To the Soul Society crew Merle, Dawn, and Karina. To all my book club women, in particular Aisling O'Toole, Ciara Clancy and Esther O'Moore Donohoe.

To my BF mums, in particular Lewine O'Connell and Karen Glackin.

To Daniella Moyles for mutual cheerleading.

To Cecelia Ahern, for advice and support.

To all my fellow 'Things Fall Aparters', who read and responded to my column and who shared their stories, thank you for your support, in particular Pam Froggatt, Ruth Griffin, Emma Blain, Wes O'Hagan, Zoe Desmond and Clare Strong.

To Paola Felix and Mirella Mubarak, for all the love you show Sarah and for being such wonderful additions in our home.

To everyone who so generously allowed me to write about them, in particular to Judith, Maria, Lou and Helen, for all your support.

To all my aunts and cousins, for support and advice, in particular Veronica and Fionnuala for showing the way.

To Nikki Cummins Black, you are as wise as you are good looking. To Rachel Lysaght, I am so lucky to be your LP. To Shereen Ibrahim, my sister from another ... To Sophie White, you are the Louise to my Louise.

To Song Yue, a constant source of support and calm. To Daragh, without whom I would be lost. To my parents, Emer and Ciarán, for everything.

To Sarah, I am the luckiest.